THE CHILD AND THE HERO

THE CHILD AND THE HERO

Coming of Age in Catullus and Vergil

MARK PETRINI

///

Ann Arbor
THE UNIVERSITY OF MICHIGAN PRESS

2000   1999   1998   1997   4   3   2   1

A CIP catalog record for this book is available from the British Library

Library of Congress Cataloging-in-Publication Data

Petrini, Mark, 1953–
    The child and the hero : coming of age in Catullus and Vergil /
Mark Petrini.
        p.   cm.
    "This book is a revision of my 1988 University of Michigan Ph.D.
dissertation."
    Includes bibliographical references and index.
    Contents: The child and the hero — Catullus — Nisus and Euryalus
— Pallas — Iulus — The art of escape and the fourth eclogue.
    ISBN 0–472–10460–8 (alk. paper)
    1. Virgil.   Aeneis.   2. Catullus, Gaius Valerius—Characters—
Children.   3. Epic poetry, Latin—History and criticism.
4. Influence (Literary, artistic, etc.) 5. Catullus, Gaius
Valerius—Influence. 6. Virgil—Knowledge—Literature. 7. Virgil—
Characters—Children. 8. Pessimism in literature. 9. Rome—In
literature.   I. Title.
PA6825.P44   1996
873'.01—DC20   96-25346
                                                       CIP

PA6825
.P44
1997

FOR MY GRANDPARENTS

ACKNOWLEDGMENTS

This book is a revision of my 1988 University of Michigan Ph.D. dissertation. Though determined to work quickly and to revise it as little as possible, I have, in long fits and starts, rewritten almost all of it, I hope to the good. It has incurred a disproportionately large burden of debt.

Family and friends have given wonderful support: thanks to Lisa Carson and Kay Young, who were there for the early innings, and to Darice Birge, Julie Ann Garey, Michael Levine, Nelson Moe, and Karen Van Dyck, who provided indispensable help during the middle and at the end of this book's preparation. Special thanks to Norman Doidge, Michael Herz, Jim Kearney, Peter Knox, Jean Roiphe, and Molly and Red, who were there throughout.

In a better world everyone would get the colleagues and the students I have had at Columbia University. I am especially grateful to Alan Cameron, Carmella Franklin, Sarah Mace, and Deborah Steiner for their energy and insights and for the pleasure I have had working with them. I would also like to thank my anonymous readers for their patience and learning; they have spared me from countless embarrassing errors and given focus and direction where I needed it most.

Thanks to my colleagues Peter Knox, James Rives, and Gareth Williams, and to Michael Herz and James O'Hara who read through drafts and talked with me about Vergil, and especially to James Zetzel, who has been a constant source of ideas and good sense. This project, finally, would never have been finished without the encouragement of Ellen Bauerle of the University of Michigan Press or without the friendship and support of James O'Hara. Greatest thanks belong to David Ross for his friendship and example.

CONTENTS

INTRODUCTION

Despite the superfluity of studies on the *Aeneid*, none has systematically examined Vergil's use of Catullus, perhaps his favorite Latin predecessor. Vergil alludes to Catullus throughout the *Eclogues*, *Georgics*, and *Aeneid*, and commentaries and articles regularly adduce individual correspondences, word by word or line by line. While such fragmentary comparisons can illuminate details of style, meter, and diction, they cannot address the fundamental (and more interesting) question of what Catullus' poetry meant to Vergil—the residual sounds and colors that remained with Vergil during a lifetime of absorbing Catullus' work. In the following pages I have focused less on the details of specific allusions and more on a pattern of borrowings, a somewhat fixed set of Catullan themes to which Vergil returns again and again as he shapes and structures his own work.

It is inevitable, given this approach, that the arguments in this book contain an imprecision and a disproportion. First, the portrait of Catullus that emerges is imprecise, more "Vergil's Catullus" than the familiar poet of the short poems, long poems, and epigrams. We have in Vergil's poetry an intellectual document of profound importance—an account of how Catullus was read by a (remarkable) near-contemporary and of the themes that spoke most insistently from his work—but one that in no sense comprehends the whole.

Second, such a study is meaningless unless grounded in a fuller reading of Vergil—a reading, furthermore, that is only partially guided by, and not limited to, Catullan allusion. Hence the disproportion: though I have given him equal billing, Catullus is necessarily discussed less often than Vergil and less often, even, than other poets to whom Vergil alludes, Homer most of all.

Surveys of Vergilian scholarship, I expect, will immediately count this book among the works of the "Harvard School," a term increasingly ill defined and certainly abused. In keeping with the current mode of confessional introductions, I admit to finding the poems of Vergil a bit melancholy and the studies by Clausen, Ross, Putnam, Zetzel, Thomas, and

O'Hara, among others, especially convincing. I do not think that every "optimistic" passage must be deconstructed for subversive subtexts or that the praises, say, of Augustus' achievements should be dismissed as insincere gestures. The debate about Vergil's supposed optimism or pessimism has too often been reduced, unreasonably and unproductively, to a narrow consideration of Augustus' status in the poems.

For the record, I have no idea what Vergil really thought of his *princeps,* and I do not think that anyone else does either. As far as the poems are concerned, they include Augustus (how could they not?) just as they include the other essential figures from poetry, myth, and history. Like Gallus, Orpheus, Daedalus, and Aeneas, Augustus struggles to create order and to keep disintegration at bay; like Vergil's other figures, Augustus sometimes succeeds (Actium) and at other times fails, often dishearteningly (Marcellus). Vergil's poetry treats these failures as local symptoms of global causes, causes embedded in human nature and in nature itself, and therefore in history. I argue in the following chapters that Vergil's figures from the political present and the mythical past all face obstacles and suffer losses that Vergil makes analogous. They all, perhaps especially Augustus, raise for the reader the same question: can any level of human intervention reconfigure these fundamental causes and redirect their momentum, change the way the future will proceed from the way the past has unfolded?

We find in Vergil's poetry unambiguous expressions of great optimism, passages that together comprise a full and sincere record of Rome's longing for poetic, scientific, and political deliverance. The headlong assumption, however, that these passages represent Vergil's conviction that deliverance is at hand is not persuasive and trivializes a complex set of oppositions. Vergil sets this record of longing against his own construction of the "facts" of politics, nature, and history, and he represents these facts as deferring or directly contradicting Roman hopes that their world will be transformed. This longing and these facts remain irreconcilably opposed almost through the end of the *Aeneid;* only Iulus offers the possibility that some reconciliation might occur. Vergil, as I argue in this book, keeps him poised on the edge of childhood, amid conflicting signs that he will either carry forward the worst features of Troy or shake free from the past and create a glorious Roman future.

CHAPTER I

The Child and the Hero

Two generations ago Eduard Fraenkel could remark that the Romans were alienated from children and childhood, even hostile to them, and expect no argument.[1] Roman social historians have long asserted the absence of "sentimental" or affective parents in antiquity: by some accounts Roman children are coldly inventoried as guarantors of family line; in philosophical terms they are half-formed creatures, imperfect versions of the adult self, and are generally deplored for their intemperance and excess.[2]

Since the 1980s a wider survey of evidence and more nuanced assessments of the sources already in play have given a fuller and somewhat different picture. While there are substantial differences from modern conceptions of childhood (particularly after Rousseau), evidence for parental affection and for interest in children does indeed appear in Roman times; moreover, it seems to increase at the end of the republic (perhaps under the influence of Augustan emphasis on "family values") and to continue to increase in the Empire.[3] We find childhood emerging as an integral period of life with its own distinct attributes, often corollaries to the negative evaluations found in the scholarship of a few generations ago.[4] It is not, accordingly, simply a time of immoderation but one of innocence, intellectual tractability, and play;[5] for some philosophical sects

1. *jugendfremd* and *jugendfeindlich;* Fraenkel 1926, 34.
2. See Ariès 1962; Veyne 1978 and 1987; Néraudau 1984, 89–97; Wiedmann 1989, 5–48; Eyben 1993. The Greeks have generally been considered more hospitable to the young: e.g., see Kassel 1951; Herter 1975, 598–619.
3. While in basic agreement, various studies have plotted the details of this evolution differently. Veyne (1978) puts its beginning in the early Empire, Manson (1978 and 1983) in the late Republic; Bradley (1987) cautions against trying to make exact assessments, given the uneven qualities and quantities of evidence. Dixon (1991) has a brief and convincing discussion of the whole issue. For children in Augustan iconography, see Néraudau 1984, 261–64, and Zanker 1988, 156–59.
4. For childhood as a distinct period of life, and for its qualities, see Néraudau 1984, 21–39, and Eyben 1993, 1–41.
5. Seneca's praise of youth represents the extreme of these views: *sic in aetate nostra quod est optimum in primo est . . . quia iuvenes possumus discere, possumus facilem animum et*

it is nature's perfect mirror,[6] even if the reflection appears in unperfected creatures. Most consistently (and most directly relevant for the following chapters), it is a "springtime" of potential in which adults invest their hopes for the future and their need for continuity with the past.[7]

Against this revised background the portraits of children in Catullus and Vergil no longer appear to be the exceptions they once seemed; both poets appropriate commonplace (though, arguably, minority) notions of childhood and elaborate them as motifs. Although the scenes of childhood and family life in Catullus' poetry have been evaluated sociologically,[8] they have received little attention as literary devices. And while previous studies of the *Eclogues, Georgics,* and *Aeneid* have discussed Vergil's child characters, they have typically focused on his apparent affection for children and on the pathos of untimely death.[9] I would like to consider childhood in a somewhat different way.

Catullus and Vergil present their young characters in transition, at the moments in which they leave childhood and enter the adult world. I will call these moments *initiations,* a term that begs some indulgence and requires some qualification. I have chosen it because it suggests the formularity and consistency that Catullus and Vergil give to these characters and to these scenes of transition, without intending to suggest the actual rituals of philosophical or religious cult. *Initiation* will stand as a synonym for "coming of age," a recurring set of images and events by which these authors mark the passing of young characters into adulthood.

Such initiations are common in literature: *virtus* (manly courage) and

---

adhuc tractabilem ad meliora convertere [so in our lifetimes, what comes first is the best . . . because when we are young we are able to learn, to train our minds to seek nobler pursuits, while they are still impressionable and still tractable.] (*Ep.* 108.26–27, cited, with discussion, in Eyben 1993, 40); see further Néraudau 1984, 99–103, 115–41.

6. Cicero *Fin.* 5.61: *pueri in quibus ut in speculis natura cernitur* [children, in whom nature appears, as if in a mirror]; for philosophers visiting nurseries, see 5.55; cf. 1.71, 5.41–45.

7. Cicero *Sen.* 19.70: *ver enim tamquam adulescentia significat ostenditque fructus futuros; reliqua autem tempora demetendis fructibus et percipiendis accomodata sunt* [for youth has the quality of springtime and shows forth the fruits that are to come; the remaining seasons are for harvesting the fruit and for reaping their rewards.] See Néraudau 1984, 98–103, and Eyben 1993, 39–41, for further sources and discussion.

8. E.g., Manson 1978, 247–91.

9. In Fraenkel's (1945) judgment, "Virgil is always at his most perfect and most characteristic when dealing with animals and young people" (5). Cf. Heinze 1915, 157–59, and Fowler 1919, 86–92. For the deaths of children see Norden 1957, *ad A.* 6.426–29 and 782 (quoted later in this chapter); Block (1980) discusses the Homeric sources for this theme; cf. also Conte 1986, 97–107.

amor (erotic love) stand, so to speak, at the threshold of adulthood, and boys grow to become heroes while girls leave their mothers' embraces for husbands and adult love. Homer's story of Telemachus is the fullest account of the heroic type: Telemachus begins the *Odyssey* as an ineffectual boy, bound to his home and mother, and emerges as a young hero making his first voyage and defending his household at his father's side.[10] His father, Odysseus, is absent and Mentor (Athena) acts as his teacher and guide. The absent father and the older guardian typify heroic training: Phoenix (or Chiron) teaches Achilles all things, "to be a speaker or a man of action" (*Il.* 9.442–43); Odysseus is initiated on a boar hunt by his grandfather Autolykos (*Od.* 19.394–466); Neoptolemus is reared by his grandfather-in-law in Skyros while Achilles fights at Troy (*Il.* 19.326), and his initiation by Odysseus is the subject of the *Philoctetes.*

As epic devices initiations are sufficiently canonical to be correspondingly reduced in so-called antiheroic poetry. Apollonius obligingly nods to the motif but reduces his "scene" to a gesture—two lines, two books apart: Lycus sends off the Argonauts with gifts and his son (*Argo.* 2.814); the son disappears from the poem until he is returned home at the end of the voyage with no word of description, not even a name (*Argo.* 4.298). The motif in literature and myth includes either extended training or an initiatory heroic act, but both versions have common elements: an absent father, an older mentor, and some process by which the values of the adult world are taught or put to the test.[11]

The heroic is only one aspect of this coming of age experience, and erotic initiations are equally typological. Nausikaa's meeting with Odysseus (*Od.* 6.110–210) is an initiation in which Homer equates childhood with a lush and remote landscape, a landscape physically and metaphorically distant from civilization and the adult world. Nausikaa plays a child's ball game and is compared to Artemis with her nymphs, while Odysseus, the agent of sexuality and experience, invades this haven from the world of deeds and wandering. The episode becomes the model for erotic initiations, and Moschus' Europa, Apollonius' Medea, and Vergil's Dido are unmistakable variations on the theme.[12] Telemachus and Nausikaa represent what one expects of maturation: a new beginning and an

10. See Klingner 1964, especially 367–68.
11. All perhaps reflect versions of real fosterage in ancient societies. The bibliography on historical fosterage is vast; e.g., Bremmer 1983 and 1978. For comment and bibliography on Rome see Hallet 1984, 164–67, 296–316.
12. And probably Calvus' Io; see Lyne 1970, *ad* 154–55. For these conventional elements see Bühler 1960, 75, 108, and Sowa 1984, 135–44.

eagerness to turn from childhood to an adulthood of love or heroism. In Catullus and Vergil this process appears with different significance.

VERGIL AND THE COMING OF AGE

Vergil treats erotic initiations via the Alexandrians and Neoterics, especially the poetry of Catullus, and he treats heroic initiations eclectically; in both cases the passing of childhood is uniformly tragic. In *Eclogue* 8 Damon sings a bitter epithalamion for Mopsus and Nysa:

> saepibus in nostris parvam te roscida mala
> (dux ego vester eram) vidi cum matre legentem.
> alter ab undecimo tum me iam acceperat annus,
> iam fragilis poteram a terra contingere ramos:
> ut vidi, ut perii, ut me malus abstulit error!

[I saw you with your mother in our orchards when you were still small, picking apples fresh with dew (I was your guide). I was just twelve years old then, just able to reach the delicate branches on tiptoe: when I saw you, how I died, what madness carried me off!]

(*Ecl.* 8.37–41)

Love ends the ease and innocence of childhood and begins the troubles of adult life.[13] Vergil separates childhood from adulthood graphically, switching Theocritean "models" in the stanza. Lines 37–38 translate closely the comic melancholy of the Cyclops' lament in *Idyll* 11:[14]

> ἠράσθην μὲν ἔγωγε τεοῦς, κόρα, ἁνίκα πρᾶτον
> ἦνθες ἐμᾷ σὺν ματρὶ θέλοισ' ὑακίνθινα φύλλα
> ἐξ ὄρεος δρέψασθαι, ἐγὼ δ' ὁδὸν ἁγεμόνευον.

---

13. Kenney (1982) says of *Ecl.* 8.37–41: "perhaps nowhere in all literature has there been captured in so brief a compass so perfect an evocation of the haunting idea of the lost paradise of childhood" (53).

14. For the tone of *Idyll* 11 and its distance from the *Pharmaceutria* (or from *Ecl.* 8) compare the further complaints by the Cyclops:

γινώσκω, χαρίεσσα κόρα, τίνος οὔνεκα φεύγεις.
οὔνεκά μοι λασία μὲν ὀφρὺς ἐπὶ παντὶ μετώπῳ
ἐξ ὠτὸς τέταται ποτὶ θώτερον ὡς μία μακρά,
εἷς δ' ὀφθαλμὸς ὕπεστι, πλατεῖα δὲ ῥὶς ἐπὶ χείλει.

[I know, sweet girl, why you flee me—because I have a single shaggy eyebrow stretched across my forehead, from one ear to the other, and one eye beneath it, and my nose lies flat on my lip.]

(*Idyll* 11.30–33)

[I fell in love with you, girl, the first time you came with my mother, wishing to pick the hyacinth leaves from the mountainside, and I showed you the way.]

(*Idyll* 11.25–27)

In line 41 Vergil changes voices, borrowing Damon's final line from Simaetha's madness in the *Pharmaceutria:*

χὼς ἴδον ὡς ἐμάνην, ὥς μοι πυρὶ θυμὸς ἰάφθη
δειλαίας, τὸ δὲ κάλλος ἐτάκετο. οὐκέτι πομπᾶς
τήνας ἐφρασάμαν, οὐδ' ὡς πάλιν οἴκαδ' ἀπῆνθον
ἔγνων, ἀλλά μέ τις καπυρὰ νόσος ἐξεσάλαξεν
κείμαν δ' ἐν κλιντῆρι δέκ' ἄματα καὶ δέκα νύκτας.

[When I saw him, how wildly I raved, how my heart burned with fire in my wretchedness, and my beauty wasted away. No longer did I watch the procession, nor know how I got home again, but a parching fever wore me utterly out, and I lay in my bed through ten days and nights.]

(*Idyll* 2.82–86)

Theocritus' Simaetha is a particular study in fatal obsession; in Vergil's poem her experience is simply what first love and adulthood mean: *ut vidi, ut perii, ut me malus abstulit error!*

This experience of adulthood has deeper implications. Contemporary Rome's decline from an idealized past is a cardinal theme of the late republic, to which Vergil applies metaphors of youth and age. Cultural "fall from innocence" is made parallel to the growth from childhood innocence to adult experience. In the fourth *Eclogue* Vergil's equations are explicit: childhood is a golden age and adulthood an iron age of warfare and blood; childhood and the golden age are literally coextensive, and the iron age emerges in stages as the *puer* grows to maturity. The fourth *Eclogue,* I will argue, challenges claims about the state of Rome in 40/39 B.C. and uses the imagery of these claims to assert that strife and pain are inevitable and that the "iron age" of heroes is nothing more than a conceit, a literary synonym for the everyday realities of life. The "golden age" of childhood is a time of passing illusions, of fantasies that, like the complementary fantasies in old age, can obscure but never change the *scelera* (crimes) and *fraudes* (treacheries) that characterize and define adulthood in the real world.[15]

15. See chapter 6. The connections between human and world ages, both in Vergil and in other ancient authors, have been noted but only briefly discussed: Dodds (1973) says that the golden age has "a deep conscious root in human experience . . . perhaps the individual experience of early infancy, when life was easy, nature supplied nourishment, and conflict did not exist" (3); see also Jachmann's passing remark (1952): "was ist diese

Rome has a different political and social climate during the period in which the *Aeneid* is composed; Vergil's epic addresses a greater variety of issues than do the *Eclogues,* and his thematic use of childhood and heroism is appropriately more elaborate and less schematic. Through the young men in the *Aeneid*—Euryalus, Pallas, Lausus, Ascanius, and Marcellus, all of whom he calls *puer*—Vergil presents the incompatible values and associations of childhood and adulthood. Child characters in the poem are made to exemplify various ideals of innocence—cultural simplicity, enduring love, *pietas,* an idealized heroic past—and they flourish briefly and die as they come of age. None of these characters is literally a boy except Ascanius, and his age is purposefully blurred (see chapter 5). *Puer* indicates a metaphoric childhood that is antithetical to and destroyed by growth to adulthood; growth is a metaphor for a "child's" introduction to warfare and to the larger world of the poem.[16]

Vergil has created this literary construct out of his own contemporary experience. In *Aeneid* 6 the shade of Anchises praises Roman posterity:

> en huius, nate, auspiciis illa incluta Roma
> imperium terris, animos aequabit Olympo,
> septemque una sibi muro circumdabit arces,
> felix prole virum: qualis Berecyntia mater
> invehitur curru Phrygias turrita per urbes
> laeta deum partu, centum complexa nepotes,
> omnis caelicolas, omnis supera alta tenentis.

[Behold, son, under Zeus' auspices glorious Rome will extend her empire to the ends of the earth, her ambitions to Olympus, and will surround her seven hills with one wall, rich in her progeny: she will be like Cybele, the Berecynthian mother, crowned with towers, carried through the cities of Phrygia in her chariot, who delights to have borne the gods, embraces a hundred grandsons, all gods, all dwelling on high.]

(A. 6.781–87)

Anchises' catalog of future heroes concludes with the shade of Marcellus (*A.* 6.868–86), Rome's favorite son and Augustus' most cherished heir; his death in 23 B.C. and Anchises' futile prayer, *si qua fata aspera rumpas, tu*

Jugend in Tat und Wahrheit? sie ist die goldene Zeit" (50); cf. Herter 1975 and Smith 1980.

16. *Puer* is not a rare word in Vergil (Wetmore [1930] lists fifty-four uses in the *Eclogues, Georgics,* and *Aeneid*) and in most cases it is used literally, as in "puerique innuptae puellae" (*A.* 6.307 = *A.* 2.238) or the *pueri* of the *lusus Troiae* (*A.* 5.545–603). It is sometimes used in Latin of young men in late adolescence (e.g., Cicero *ad Fam.* 12.25.4); Vergil uses the word thematically with other, more emphatic, suggestions of childhood, to mark the transition to adulthood (see, e.g., on Euryalus, "Boy and Man" in chapter 3).

Marcellus eris [If only you can break the bonds of fate, if only . . . ; you will be Marcellus] (*A.* 6.882–83),[17] belie the promise of Roman fecundity. Norden's note gives the proper historical corrective:

> Wenn man bedenkt, dass die Bestrebungen des Augustus *de augende prole* anfingen, als Vergil mit der Aeneis begann, und durch eine *lex Iulia* ihren Abschluss fanden, als er sie beendete, wird man das Pathos der Worte nachfuhlen.[18]

Norden refers to a chronic problem in the republic, the declining birthrate among the Roman nobility, the inability of the upper classes even to maintain their numbers.[19] History records a long tradition of responses to the problem: in 131 B.C. the censor Metellus Macedonicus urged the senate to replenish the patrician ranks by making marriage compulsory, *de augenda prole;* Cicero exhorted Caesar to encourage childbearing among native Romans, *propaganda suboles* (*pro Marcello* 23, cf. *Leg.* 3.7); Augustus, in turn, took up the challenge, reading Metellus' speech in the senate, and later publishing it as an edict. Augustus went farther, and the *lex Iulia* of 18 B.C. (the year after Vergil's death) penalized bachelors, required widows to remarry within six months, and restricted the inheritances of childless couples—all for nothing: the effect was apparently slight and the outcry overwhelming. A generation later, with the decline still unchecked, the *lex Papia Poppaea* (A.D. 9) continued the program of the *lex Iulia,* though with milder sanctions.[20]

The deaths of children in the *Aeneid* are not mere pathos, nor are they only individual losses and particular tragedies. They represent the loss of renewal, both in the time of the narrative and in republican Rome. No less than the civil wars or the proscriptions and bloodshed of the 40s, Rome's lost power of growth and lost hope of renewal are presented as symptoms of a systemic affliction, located by Vergil in Troy and in Rome's founding, and doomed to repetition; though the seemingly endless civil wars had finally ended, their ancestral causes remained and would someday produce the symptoms again.[21] The *Aeneid* gives an eti-

---

17. See Shackelton Bailey 1986 for discussion and translation of this line.

18. Norden 1957, *ad A.* 6.781; and for Marcellus, see "Marcellus and *Romana potens*" in chapter 5.

19. See Hopkins 1983, 69–107.

20. See Brunt 1987, 131–55, 558–66; Treggiari 1991, 57–80.

21. Pollio, writing from Spain after the battle of Mutina, grieves for his generation wasted by civil war: *quo si qui laetantur in praesentia, quia videntur et duces et veterani Caesaris partium interisse, tamen postmodo necesse est doleant cum vastitatem Italiae respexerint. nam et robur et suboles militum interit* (Pollio *ad Fam.* 10.33.1, cited in Syme 1939, 174 n. 3).

ology for the failures of the *Eclogues*, the *spes gregis* born only to die on bare rock:[22]

> en ipse, capellas
> protinus aeger ago; hanc etiam vix, Tityre, duco.
> hic inter densas corylos modo namque gemellos,
> spem gregis, a! silice in nuda conixa reliquit.

[Look, sick as I am, I must force my goats onward, and I can scarcely drive this one: for she, giving birth on bare stone, has just now abandoned her kids, a pair of them, there in the hazel thicket. Alas! the future of the flock.]

(*Ecl.* 1.12–15)

And in Vergil's epic the ruling principle of the *Georgics* remains unchanged:[23]

> sic omnia fatis
> in peius ruere ac retro sublapsa referri,
> non aliter quam qui adverso vix flumine lembum
> remigiis subigit, si bracchia forte remisit,
> atque illum in praeceps prono rapit alveus amni.

[So all things are fated to worsen and decay, and, as they fail, to slip ever toward decline: no differently than the rower who, driving with his oars, scarcely keeps his boat in place against the current, and if he slacken at all, the river sweeps him headlong downstream.]

(*G.* 1.199–203)

Actium, the end of civil war, and the evolving Augustan program may produce an ordered world, just as the Trojans produce (by some accounts) a miracle of civilization in the wilderness of Latium, but social and political gains do nothing to affect either human realities or the forces of nature. Without renewal there can be no hope, no change, no escape from the patterns of history.

Cf. the frequent laments for the hopelessness of escape from Rome's afflictions—e.g., Horace *Epod.* 16 and Vergil *Georgics* 1.501–14.

22. Servius is aware of this theme: *ad A.* 2.504 he glosses *spes tanta nepotum*, the fifty bedrooms of Priam's sons falling in ruins on the last night of Troy, with the lost *spem gregis* of *Ecl.* 1.15. (Note: all references to Servius' commentary throughout this book are to the 1881–84 edition listed in the bibliography.)

23. See Ross 1987, especially 234–42, and Thomas 1988b, *ad loc.*

THE EPIC WORLD AND ROME

The successes and failures of Euryalus, Pallas, Lausus, and Iulus inevitably define the world of Vergil's epic, a world with new rules and values that require some definition. It is simpler to say what the *Aeneid* is not than to say what it is. When in Book 2 Aeneas fails to persuade Anchises to leave the ruins of Troy, he resolves to return to battle and die a hero's death:

> arma, viri, ferte arma; vocat lux ultima victos.
> reddite me Danais; sinite instaurata revisam
> proelia. numquam omnes hodie moriemur inulti.

[To arms, men, to arms: the conquered are called to take their final stand. Let me face the Greeks again and see the fighting renewed. On no account will all of us this day die unavenged.]

(*A.* 2.668–70)

Aeneas uses the gestures of Homer's most famous exit, Hector from Andromache (*Il.* 6.369–502),[24] and his diction is heroic in the grand style: Vergil quotes the beginning of his own poem, *arma viri*,[25] archaizes with the repetition *arma . . . arma*,[26] and concludes with a cliché sufficiently shopworn to be parodied by Plautus (*Amph.* 1041)[27] and by Horace in the *Satires* (2.8.34).[28] These tired phrases and heroic poses are far from Vergil's Iliadic "model," the convincing and human portrait of Hector; and in place of Andromache's dignity and quiet grief, we find Creusa clinging to her husband in the doorway—*complexa pedes in limine coniunx* (*A.* 2.673)—and begging, quite reasonably, that he protect her life and their home (*A.* 2.675–77). This is obviously not straight Homer, but neither is it parody or melodrama. In the *Aeneid* heroic behavior (as it appears in the Homeric poems) becomes mannered and empty gestures, and epic *topoi* no longer give substance or meaning to characters and their world. Aeneas fails to convince as Hector, just as he fails to convince as Odysseus

---

24. Compared by Forbiger (1872–75, vol. 2) and Conington (1963), *ad loc.*; see Knauer 1964, 381.

25. For the motif see Norden 1957, 368 n. 2, with Bloch 1970 and Weber 1987.

26. Fraenkel (1945, 6 n. 9) notes the antiquity and tone of this repetition.

27. Compared by Austin (1964), *ad A.* 4.670: *numquam edepol me inultus istic ludificabit, quisquis est* [never, by god, will that man make a fool of me with impunity, no matter who he is].

28. *nos nisi damnose bibimus, moriemur inulti* [Unless we drink him to his ruin, we will die unavenged]; see Norden 1957, *ad A.* 6.836 for discussion; Forbiger (1872–75, vol. 2) and Heyne (1830–42, vol. 3), *ad loc.*, compare *Il.* 22.304–5.

or Achilles; more important, neither Hector nor Odysseus nor Achilles (as exemplars of Homeric failures and strengths) fits easily in the world of the *Aeneid.*

More precisely, Vergil presents the ideals and tokens of conventional heroism—*spolia, laudes, virtus*—as illusions that betray and deceive in an inverted heroic world. The opening words of the poem establish this program: Servius (*ad A.* 1.1) remarks on the chiasmus created by *arma, virum,* and the *"Iliad"* and *"Odyssey"* halves of the *Aeneid: nam prius de erroribus Aeneae dicit, post de bello* [For Vergil speaks first about the wanderings of Aeneas and then about the war]. This chiasmus is not just rhetorical elegance: *arma virum* suggests that Vergil's epic will evolve like the sequence of the Homeric poems, that *Odyssey* will follow *Iliad,* that *furor* and strife will resolve into peace, and that warfare and heroic deeds will give way to love, home, and family. The *Aeneid,* in fact, offers no such consolations, and the promise of the opening words is false (the first deception in the poem): after long and perilous wandering the new Odysseus arrives in another Troy to begin a second *Iliad.* Vergil's world is disordered, without final respite and without hope of the eventual escape from suffering and pain that the sequence of the *Iliad* and the *Odyssey* predicts.

In creating his epic world Vergil saw possibilities that Propertius, for example, did not. Propertius, were he ever to write a heroic poem, would record the deeds of Caesar and Maecenas—Mutina, Philippi, Egypt, and Actium (2.1.25-34)—and would ignore myth and distant times:

> non ego Titanas canerem, non Ossan Olympo
> impositam, ut caeli Pelion esset iter,
> nec veteres Thebas, nec Pergama nomen Homeri
> Xerxis et imperio bina coisse vada,
> regnave prima Remi aut animos Carthaginis altae,
> Cimbrorumque minas et bene facta Mari.

[I would not sing of Titans, or of Ossa stacked on Olympus so that Pelion could be a path to the heavens; nor would I sing of ancient Thebes, or Troy (Homer's fame), or the twin seas joined by the command of Xerxes; nor even the first kingdom of Remus, or the insolence of lofty Carthage, and the threats of the Cimbri, and the great deeds of Marius.]

(2.1.19-24)

The conventional rejection of theogonic and Homeric poetry is extended even to the Roman past (*regna . . . Remi . . . facta Mari*), suggesting the urgency with which recent events and current realities demand attention and explication. Vergil's profession in the third *Georgic—mox tamen arden-*

tis accingar dicere pugnas / Caesaris [soon I will prepare myself to sing the fiery battles of Caesar] (G. 3.46–77)—reflects the same urgency, and the only surprise may be that it took so long for a poem on the civil wars to appear. In such a climate a foundation epic was not Vergil's most obvious choice,[29] and he reclaims and legitimates remote antiquity by reading Roman history backward: the disorder and chaos of his own lifetime, the *ardentis . . . pugnas Caesaris,* and the fact of chronic lost posterity are the raw materials from which he creates Trojan and Latin antiquity.

In the following chapters I argue that Catullus is Vergil's indispensable model for this conflation of the mythical and the real. The same "subjectivity"[30] that Catullus brings to epyllion, epigram, and even translation Vergil brings to epic, and for the same reason: the age of heroes in Catullus 64 and the world of Troy are not *like* Catullus' own; they *are* his own. Troy is the *commune sepulchrum Asiae Europaeque* and more:

> Troia virum et virtutum omnium acerba cinis,
> quaene etiam nostro letum miserabile fratri
> attulit . . .
>
> quem nunc tam longe non inter nota sepulcra
> nec prope cognatos compositum cineres
> sed Troia obscena, Troia infelice sepultum
> detinet extremo terra aliena solo.
> ad quam tum properans fertur <lecta> undique pubes
> Graeca penetralis deseruisse focos
> ne Paris abducta gavisus libera moecha
> otia pacato degeret in thalamo.
> quo tibi tum casu, pulcerrima Laudamia,

---

29. Vergil seems to have considered an epic blending the Trojan past and Roman present early on: at the beginning of the third *Georgic* he promises to build Caesar a temple (i.e., a poem) that will include the events of recent history, the trophies of Egypt and the Parthians, as well as the events of mythic antiquity: *[stabunt] Assaraci proles demissaeque ab Iove gentis / nomina, Trosque parens et Troiae Cynthius auctor* [images of the offspring of Assaracus, and the names of the people descended from Zeus, and father Tros and Cynthian Apollo, founder of Troy <will stand> about the temple] (G. 3.35–36). On possible anticipations of the *Aeneid* in the *Georgics* see Thomas 1988b, *ad* G. 3.46–47 and pp. 1–3.

30. This term, the standard critical term for Catullus' practice of thoroughly shaping figures and genres to the concerns of his own life and times, can be applied equally usefully to Vergil's epic if it is applied only in this sense. Otis' (1963) discussion of "subjective epic" contains many acute remarks but perhaps overburdens the word with too many meanings.

ereptum est vita dulcius atque anima
coniugium.

[Troy, the bitter grave of all men and all manhood, which also brought
my brother a pitiable death . . . my brother whom now a foreign land de-
tains at the ends of the earth, laid to rest far away, neither among familiar tombs nor near his family's graves, but who is buried at Troy, Troy
the foul and accursed. To Troy, they say, the <picked> youths from all of
Greece sped off and left their hearths and homes, in order that Paris not
spend his days at ease in his bed, away from battle, delighting in his
stolen adulteress. By that disaster, beautiful Laudamia, your husband,
sweeter to you than life and breath, was torn from you.]

(68.90–92, 97–107)

Mythical tragedy is not simply a model for miseries in the present. Troy
is a timeless conceit for treachery and loss in which Laudamia and Catullus, Protesilaus and Catullus' brother, play interchangeable roles: the
sufferings of the past are included among and indistinguishable from the
sorrows of the present. Vergil's poem is equally the poetry of current reality, life as Vergil and his contemporaries experience it: the people and
events from the mythical past are made to provide insistent demonstra-
tions of the realities of his own age.

CHAPTER II

Catullus

Either Lesbia's love is pure and friends are unfailing in a perfect world, or Catullus languishes alone in a barren place as Lesbia takes lovers by the hundreds. Life in Catullus' poetry tends to be starkly polar, buried in gloom or brilliantly lit, almost never anything in between. The affair with Lesbia is but one of the many dramas through which Catullus expresses these polarities, and all are complementary: in poem 64 an innocent age, before the *Argo*, opposes Troy and the ruined present; in 63 home and identity give way to exile and utter loss of self; in other poems perfect lovers are torn from their beloved (66, 68, etc.). Catullus also conforms childhood and adulthood to this paradigm of oppositions; this feature is striking and seems to have held special attraction and significance for Vergil. Some general remarks here will prepare the way for the detailed discussions of Euryalus, Pallas, and Iulus in chapters 3–5.

Catullus presents childhood as an ideal state of innocence and love that is inevitably destroyed as the child grows up and becomes corrupted by the infidelities that pervade adult life—adulthood defined, of course, by Catullus' (alleged) experiences of Lesbia, Alfenus (poem 30), and others, the whole cast of the faithless. Poem 65, for example, depends on the antithesis between childhood and adulthood, and the purportedly disparate parts of the poem (Troy, the death of Catullus' brother, Hortalus, and the *Coma Berenices*) are unified by the concluding simile. Catullus sends Hortalus the Callimachus translation he has promised,

> ne tua dicta vagis nequiquam credita ventis
> efflluxisse meo forte putes animo,
> ut missum sponsi furtivo munere malum
> procurrit casto virginis e gremio,
> quod miserae oblitae molli sub veste locatum,
> dum adventu matris prosilit, excutitur,
> atque illud prono praeceps agitur decursu,
> huic manat tristi conscius ore rubor.

[lest by chance you think that your words have fled from my mind, entrusted / in vain to the wandering winds, like an apple, sent as a furtive gift from a lover, / rolls forth from a maiden's chaste lap; hidden and forgotten beneath the soft / dress of the unhappy girl, it falls out as she jumps up startled at her mother's / approach; the apple rolls out, and a guilty blush spreads over the girl's sad face.]

(65.17–24)

This image has been called Alexandrian in inspiration or, more precisely, Callimachean, and interpretations and commentaries have tended to stop with these formal assessments.[1] Fordyce, for example, concludes that the lines are a preface to the "gallant court poetry" of poem 66, which relieves the gloom of the preceding lines.[2] It would be surprising, however, for such an elaborate conceit to have so little purpose; and what of its relationship to the preceding lines, surely the proper focus of any discussion of the simile's meaning?

The change in the *virgo*'s life is the drama as well as the theme of the simile: her innocence and isolation (*casto gremio*) yield to maturity and the life of *amor*, with its inevitable deceptions (*furtivo munere*) and unhappiness (*tristi . . . ore*).[3] By her lover's gift and by her deception of her mother she has lost (like Ariadne in poem 64) the fundamental bond of childhood, the trust and sympathy between mother and daughter, and she acknowledges her violation (*conscius rubor*). The meaning of the simile, therefore, emerges obliquely, beyond the strict logic of its *tertium comparationis*,[4] and is more typically Catullan than its form or antecedents suggest. Catullus asserts that his pledge to Hortalus will not be violated by "betrayal" and neglect, and that, unlike the *virgo*, Catullus and his *amicitia* will remain "innocent," uncompromised by the negligence and faithlessness that pervade the world at large. The lines introducing the simile now have more point:

> ne tua dicta vagis nequiquam credita ventis
> effluxisse meo forte putes animo.

(65.17–18)

This *topos* is a kind of formula in Catullus for promises not kept and

---

1. Kroll (1968, *ad loc.*) compares Callimachus' Acontius and Cydippe; see also Fordyce 1961, *ad loc.* For discussions of form and theme see Wilamowitz-Moellendorf 1924, 304–5 (for whom the simile is inspired by Apollonius), and especially Clausen 1970.

2. Fordyce 1961, 325.

3. Cf. Catullus 68.145, where *furtiva munuscula* is a metaphor for Lesbia's "gift" of clandestine love.

4. Quinn 1970, 354: "surely the apple stands for the version itself [of the *Coma Berenices*] which Catullus had been working on when his brother's death caused him to put it aside."

trusts violated: those of Theseus (64.139–42) and those of Alfenus (30.9–10).[5] Here the image draws attention to the polarities in poem 65 that typify so much of Catullus' poetry. On one side are the guilelessness and innocence of youth, the responsibilities of *amicitia* dutifully met,[6] and familial love—the one kind of love exempt from the usual depredations of *eros:*

> Dicebas quondam solum te nosse Catullum,
> Lesbia, nec prae me velle tenere Iovem.
> dilexi tum te non tantum ut vulgus amicam,
> sed pater ut gnatos diligit et generos.

[You used to tell me, Lesbia, that you knew no man but me, and that you would not / trade my embrace for Jupiter's. / I loved you then not only as any man loves his / lover, but as a father loves his sons and sons-in-law.]

(72.1–4)

On the other side are faithless love, friendships betrayed, and the separation of death, with Troy as their constant exemplum (68.90–107, quoted in chapter 1).

This interpretation extends to the poem that follows. Michael Putnam has suggested that Catullus' translation of the *Coma Berenices* is more than "gallant court poetry" and that poem 66, though a translation, is yet another vehicle for the ruling passions of so much of Catullus' verse—anxiety and remorse at infidelities and loss.[7] Wendell Clausen discusses 65 and 66 together (though not this theme of the concluding simile), interpreting Catullus' sadness at his brother's death (65.5–14) and its generalization to Troy and to the endemic betrayals of modern life as a prelude to the lock's grief at her separation in the poem that follows: *invita,*

5. With the promises of faithless Alfenus, *idem nunc retrahis te ac tua dicta omnia factaque / ventos irrita ferre ac nebulas aerias sinis* (30.9–10), compare Ariadne's lament:

> at non haec quondam blanda promissa dedisti
> voce mihi, non haec miseram sperare iubebas,
> sed conubia laeta, sed optatos hymenaeos,
> quae cuncta aerii discerpunt irrita venti.

[But these were not the promises you once made to me with seductive words, nor did you bid me to expect this fate in my wretchedness, but a joyful marriage, and the wedding that I longed for—all promised in vain, all scattered on the wind.]

(64.139–42)

6. For the oppositions contained in poem 30 and for *amicitia* generally see Ross 1969, 80–93.

7. Putnam 1970a.

o regina, tuo de vertice cessi (66.39).[8] The simile provides the final step in this argument: the end of the sympathies and innocence of childhood and the beginnings of adult love are precisely what the lock laments and what Berenice's marriage will bring.[9]

In another wedding poem, 64, we find the same focus on lost innocence—Ariadne's and, analogously, the world's after the Argo; in composing 64 Catullus no doubt took special note that Callimachus' lock compares her own plight with that of the catasterized Ariadne (Call. *Aetia* 4 frag. 110.59–65; cf. Catullus 66.59–61). Catullus clusters image upon image of treachery and death, for which the marriage of Peleus and Thetis is both a cause and an emblem: their union arises from the voyage of the Argo, the first ship in the world, which signals the end of innocence and the beginning of a rather idiosyncratic "iron age"; their coverlet, embroidered with scenes from the story of Theseus and Ariadne, lingers on the girl's abandonment once she has been lured away from her home and family. In the final quarter of the poem the Parcae sing the consequences of their marriage: first Troy, the beginning of warfare and strife among men and discord between the gods, then the usual hallmarks of a world in decline—brother killing brother, fathers praying for the deaths of their sons, justice and piety vanishing from the earth:

> sed postquam tellus scelere est imbuta nefando
> iustitiamque omnes cupida de mente fugarunt,
> perfudere manus fraterno sanguine fratres,
> destitit extinctos natus lugere parentes,
> optavit genitor primaevi funera nati,
> liber uti nuptae poteretur flore novellae,
> ignaro mater substernens se impia nato
> impia non verita est divos scelerare penates.

[But after the earth was steeped in unspeakable crime and all men banished / thoughts of justice from minds bent only on desire, then brothers stained their / hands in brothers' blood, the son ceased to mourn his parents' death, the father / hoped for the death of his firstborn, so that

---

8. Vergil, at any rate, took the lock's grief seriously, making Aeneas quote its lament to Dido's shade: *invitus, regina, tuo de litore cessi* (*A.* 6.460). See Clausen 1970, 90–92, for the interpretation of these passages. Clausen's article is still the *prolegendum* for any interpretation of Catullus and Vergil.

9. Putnam 1970a, 226: "indeed, it can only be the poet's deep involvement in the theme of separation which impelled him to write [the digression of lines 75–88]." This interpretation of the poem is valid, as Clausen (1970) makes clear, whether or not these lines really do digress from Callimachus' text.

he could freely enjoy the bloom / of his son's new bride. The impious mother lies with her son, he unaware of his / crime, she too impious to fear her offense to the familial gods.]

(64.397–404)

Marriage, one of Catullus' chief metaphors for this failure of innocence and this pathology of adulthood (as in poems 64, 65, and 66), is presented as the quintessential transition from youth to maturity and as the dissolution of home and family. The implied distinctions in poems 64, 65, and 66 between innocence and experience, familial love and *eros,* and the child's world and adulthood are explicit in the *epithalamia.* Poems 61 and 62 are highly mannered, composed of an inherited body of figures and diction,[10] yet even here, as in the *Coma Berenices,* where we expect Catullus to be the most constrained by form and least in character, the essential preoccupations of his verse nevertheless appear. The *raptus* of the young bride and the mock violence of her separation from family, home, and childhood itself become more than learned conventions; Catullus presents them as genuinely violent and tragic because they bring an end to innocence and lead to adult love.

The skill with which Catullus uses the *topoi* and conceits of traditional epithalamia tends to obscure this sense in his poems; we can recognize it chiefly by its persistence.[11] The apostrophe to the *concubinus* in 61, for example, is partly the mocking banter we expect in this genre, as the master's favorite is cast aside for the bride, but Catullus' diction suggests real sadness as well:

> ne diu taceat procax
> Fescennina iocatio,
> nec nuces pueris neget
> desertum domini audiens
>   concubinus amorem.
> da nuces pueris, iners,
> concubine: satis diu
> lusisti nucibus: lubet
> iam servire Talasio.
>   concubinus, nuces da.
> sordebant tibi vilicae,
> concubine, hodie atque heri;

---

10. Fraenkel 1955 and Fedeli 1981; Fedeli provides a thorough discussion of the genre's traditional elements.

11. See the comments of Klingner 1964, 216–17, and Commager 1983, 21–33.

> nunc tuum cinerarius
> tondet os. miser a miser
> concubine, nuces da.

[Let the lively Fescennine songs not be silent for long, and let the master's / favorite not refuse nuts to the boys when he hears that his master's / love for him / has ended. Now give away your nuts, idler, beloved one; you have played with / them long enough: you must now serve Talassius. Until today the country girls / seemed worthless to you: now the barber crops your hair. O pitiable, pitiable / lover, give away your nuts.]

(61.121–33)

Manlius' marriage means the end of boyish love (in this case, homosexual) and the *concubinus* is forced into (heterosexual) adulthood, jokingly obliged to accept the rustic women he formerly scorned (*sordebant . . . os*). Catullus uses neoteric *a* with *miser* elsewhere (of Attis at 63.61) to describe anguish and regret at calamitous change, and *a* typically occurs in erotic laments of stricken lovers, most notably of Calvus' Io (frag. 9) and of Catullus' Ariadne (64.71, 135).[12] The interjection here suggests the change and loss that Manlius' marriage will bring to the *concubinus*: childhood must end (*satis diu / lusisti nucibus*),[13] and adulthood must begin, accompanied, as usual, by desertion (*desertum domini audiens / concubinus amorem*).

Children, lovers, brides, and grooms will inevitably relive (as Catullus himself claims that he has with Lesbia) the experience of Theseus and Ariadne, Laodamia and Protesilaus,[14] and the other paradigmatic sufferers in Catullus' world. The antithesis between childhood and adulthood, and the values and associations of each, are among the controlling themes of Catullus' poetry; Catullan images of the separation and betrayals that accompany the end of childhood and the beginning of adult life are introduced by Vergil to gloss the "children" of the *Aeneid*, their transition to adulthood, and the character of their world.

---

12. See Ross 1969, 51–53, for discussion and further examples.

13. In sculpture and art children are often shown playing with nuts—e.g., see Eyben 1993, plate 4b. For nuts as toys see Fedeli 1981, 88–90; Néraudau 1984, 295–96; cf. Servius *ad Ecl.* 8.30.

14. Cf. Elder 1951, 126–36.

CHAPTER III

Nisus and Euryalus

While few critics would now accept that the episode of Nisus and Eury-alus represents a "juvenile epyllion" that Vergil later adapted to the *Aeneid*, it is still tempting to treat the episode as a digression, a "romantic adventure" independent of the rest of the poem, with separate themes and a detachable, instructive, moral.[1] The episode is indeed self-contained: Vergil introduces his characters in Book 9 as if for the first time, despite their appearance in Book 5; the mission ends in their deaths, and Vergil's anthemic apostrophe seems an obvious closure.[2] Despite this structural separateness, the themes discussed in chapters 1 and 2 will allow us to treat the episode as a nucleus rather than as an appendage, as a concentration of the themes of childhood and adulthood in particular and those of the second half of the poem in general. Euryalus' initiation is, first of all, the centerpiece of the fundamental initiation narrative in the *Aeneid*, that of Pallas by Aeneas in Books 8 and 10. Vergil, moreover, makes his episode arise naturally and almost inevitably from the issues of the Trojan settlement in Italy—the propagation, that is, of the features of the Trojan past in the new world, features that, transplanted in Latium, have significant implications for the Roman future.

BOY AND MAN

To begin with an obvious but essential point, Euryalus is not a boy; Vergil makes his childhood thematic rather than literal.[3] He has grown up at war, been trained in combat (*A*. 9.201–4), and routinely fights at Nisus'

---

1. Mendell (1951, 216–19) discusses and rejects the arguments for the episode as an independent composition.

2. *A*. 9.446–49; see "The Initiation of Euryalus" in chapter 3. The vengeful mutilation of the bodies of Nisus and Euryalus and the lament by Euryalus' mother that follow Vergil's eulogy (*A*. 9.450–502) are transitional, returning us from the episode proper to the main narrative.

3. Compare with the passages emphasizing Euryalus' youth, his brief but impressive *aristeia* (*A*. 9.342–51).

side: *his amor unus erat, pariterque in bella ruebant* [they shared a common love and went side by side into battle] (*A.* 9.182).[4] Euryalus is a seasoned, if young, warrior at the beginning of adulthood, *ora puer prima signans intonsa iuventa* [a boy showing first down on his unshaven cheeks] (*A.* 9.181), at the age when heroic promise begins to show.[5]

Vergil nevertheless emphasizes his youth and inexperience, first by using the word *puer*: Euryalus is always called *puer* before the mission begins (*A.* 9.181, 217, 276) but never after, even at the moment when his own helplessness and Nisus' concern to protect him are most evident, *qua vi iuvenem, quibus audeat armis / eripere?* [by what effort, by what arms could he free the young man?] (*A.* 9.399–400).[6] Second, this metaphor of childhood is extended by the prominence of Euryalus' mother and by the love between mother and son.[7] Euryalus cannot face her before he leaves: *nequeam lacrimas perferre parentis* [I could not endure my mother's tears] (*A.* 9.289), and he asks as his only reward that she be protected if he should not return (*A.* 9.290–92). She, in turn, could not bear to leave him and refused to remain either at Troy or at the settlement for the other *matres* in Sicily (*A.* 9.284–86). Her love for him is the final and strongest argument in Nisus' attempt to persuade Euryalus to stay behind:

> neu matri miserae tanti sim causa doloris
> quae te sola, puer, multis e matribus ausa
> persequitur, magni nec moenia curat Acestae.

[Nor would I be the cause of such grief for your mother: she alone of all the mothers dared to follow you, boy, and gave no thought to great Acestes' walls.]

(*A.* 9.216–18)

---

4. Servius (*ad A.* 9.178), seems misled by the effectiveness of Vergil's suggestions of youthful innocence: "*Euryalus quo pulchrior alter / non fuit Aeneadum Troiana neque induit arma* [*A.* 9.180–81]": *hoc est qui nondum bellicosa arma induerat* ["Euryalus, than whom none of the Aeneadae were more noble, nor had any more noble ever put on Trojan arms": he means he had never yet worn arms for battle].

5. Evander and Pallas first encounter the heroic world at this same age: *tum mihi prima genas vestibat flore iuventas, / mirabarque duces Teucros* [Then first flower of youthful down cloaked my cheeks, and I gazed in wonder at the Trojan leaders] (*A.* 8.160–61). Conington compares *Od.* 11.319.

6. *Puerum* and *iuvenem* are metrically equivalent in this position and could have been used interchangeably, further suggesting that they are not casual variants.

7. In Catullus 65 the relationship between mother and daughter defines the *virgo*'s childhood, in contrast to the adult (erotic) love a young girl feels for her *sponsus*; see chapter 2.

Euryalus, finally, is closely associated with Iulus, who really is a child, and who promises to protect Euryalus' mother (as a surrogate son) if the mission fails: *namque erit ista mihi genetrix nomenque Creusae / solum defuerit* [for she will be a mother to me and only lack the name Creusa] (*A.* 9.297–98).[8] Only Nisus is offered gifts for his part in the mission, an adult whose world and values Iulus attempts (unsuccessfully) to imitate. Iulus promises Euryalus friendship, one boy to another:

> te vero, mea quem spatiis propioribus aetas
> insequitur, venerande puer, iam pectore toto
> accipio et comitem casus complector in omnis.

> [But you, admirable boy, whom my own age follows more nearly, I receive you now with all my heart and embrace you as a companion in every turn of fortune.]
>
> (*A.* 9.275–77)

Vergil builds the episode on the polarity of childhood and adulthood, and he presents Euryalus as a character in transition, from childhood to the epic world of the poem. The boy is attracted by heroic adventure, *magno laudum percussus amore* [struck by great love of praise] (*A.* 9.197), and must decide between the rewards of heroism and his filial love and obligations.[9] Behind him lies, implicitly, the innocence of childhood itself; what await him are the ideals that Nisus embodies—adult heroism, *fama*, and *laudes*.

True to the typology of initiations, Euryalus' father is absent (perhaps dead), and Nisus is his initiator. This typology implies that Nisus will guide and teach the younger man, while instilling in him the values that the adult world both approves and requires for survival; once initiated the boy will take a man's role beside other heroes.[10] Nisus is a complex

---

8. Euryalus' concern for his mother matches Iulus' for Aeneas: Aeneas is the focus of all Iulus' hope and effort—[*mihi*] *sola salus genitore reducto* [(my) happiness is with my father returned to me] (*A.* 9.257)—and Vergil stresses the bond between father and son: *revocate parentem, / reddite conspectum; nihil illo triste recepto* [summon my father, return him to my sight; with him recovered, nothing can be sad] (*A.* 9.261–62).

9. Compare again Vergil's portrait of Euryalus with Catullus' *virgo* in poem 65 (see chapter 2), where childhood is the notional world of innocence, of love, and of connection to family that the child must leave behind. For the same tension elsewhere in the *Aeneid* compare Venus' love for Iulus, *positis inglorius armis / exigat hic aevum* (*A.* 10.52–53); see Heinze 1915, 269–70, and Kosthorst 1934, 90–94.

10. Telemachus, e.g.: he embarks on a miniature *Odyssey* to Pylos and Sparta, guided by Mentes (Athena) while his father is away; he returns to fight beside Odysseus, confirmed that he is his father's son. See "The Child and the Hero" in chapter 1.

and original creation, in whom Vergil combines an eclectic assortment of heroic attributes. Nisus is first introduced in Book 9 by epithet, patronym, and homeland, the full complement of a Homeric soldier:

> Nisus erat portae custos, acerrimus armis
> Hyrtacides, comitem Aeneae quem miserat Ida
> venatrix iaculo celerem levibusque sagittis.

[Nisus was posted at the gate, he the son of Hyrtacus, exceedingly fierce in arms, whom Ida, the huntress, had sent to accompany Aeneas; he was quick with the spear and with light arrows.]

(*A.* 9.176–78)

His fighting is described as a lion's attack (*A.* 9.339–41), and his abiding interest is praise: *nam mihi facti / fama sat est* [for myself, to be known for the deed is reward enough] (*A.* 9.194–95). He is appropriately restless in peace and eager for glory:

> dine hunc ardorem mentibus addunt
> Euryale, an sua cuique deus fit dira cupido?
> aut pugnam aut aliquid iamdudum invadere magnum
> mens agitat mihi, nec placida contenta quiete est.

[Do the gods, Euryalus, give hearts this passion, or does each man's strongest desire become a god? For some time now my heart urges me to do battle or to attempt some great deed, nor can it endure untroubled peace.]

(*A.* 9.184–87)

Nisus is nevertheless more than a standard-issue Homeric hero: he and Euryalus are approximately in the roles of ἐραστής and ἐρόμενος, "lover" and "beloved," a Greek version (or more precisely, a fifth-century Athenian version) of fosterage and initiation. According to Pausanias in Plato's *Symposium* (the most familiar account) the love between a younger and an older man spurs each to greatness, the former out of desire to imitate, the latter from a desire to please and instruct. What source Vergil directly or indirectly follows (whether specifically Plato or a general tradition) is less important than his modifications. For Pausanias the ἐραστής/ἐρόμενος relationship is sexual; the relationship between Nisus and Euryalus seems explicitly "Platonic": *Euryalus forma insignis viridique iuventa, / Nisus amore pio pueri* [Euryalus was known for his beauty and budding manhood; Nisus for his pious love of the boy] (*A.* 5.295–96). Vergil's modification is perhaps decorous impreision (they really are lovers, but Vergil is tactfully vague);[11] more likely, it is a precisely drawn and original assimilation of certain Greek aristocratic ideals to contemporary idealizations of early Rome. Sallust, for example, describes the rigor and austerity of primitive Roman youth in terms not far from those Vergil uses of Nisus, especially their desire to excel in the sight of their companions: *se quisque hostem ferire, murum ascendere, conspici, dum tale facinus faceret, properabat* [each man strove to lay low an enemy, to scale a wall, and, while in the very act, to be seen doing it] (*Cat.* 7.6).[12] He summarizes their greatness with a single memorable phrase, *virtus omnia domuerat* [manly courage had brought all things under its sway] (*Cat.* 7.6). The particular function of *eros* in the Greek tradition for the training and initiating of young men by their elders is changed to *pius amor,* and so is accomodated to the ideals and values of early Rome.

There is still more to this characterization: Nisus wears a lion's pelt, *pellem horrentis leonis* (*A.* 9.306), which, with his huntress mother *Ida venatrix,*[13] and his skill with arrows, further suggests the primitive *virtus* of Heracles (as told by Evander) and especially of Camilla.[14] The suggestion of primitivism attributes to Nisus commonplaces about precivilized innocence, familiar in part from idealized notions of the Roman past, an age of virtue before contemporary dissipation and moral decline.[15]

THE INITIATION OF EURYALUS

Vergil has set the stage: Euryalus leaves his childhood of love and dependency for heroic manhood, professing his attraction to these ideals in true heroic idiom:

> est hic, est animus lucis contemptor et istum
> qui vita bene credat emi, quo tendis, honorem.

11. Lee (1980) argues (wrongly, in my opinion) that their relationship is sexual: "Virgil was . . . making a statement on homosexual relationships" (111); for the arguments and bibliography see Hardie 1994, 31–34.

12. Compare further their disregard for rewards: *sed gloriae maximum certamen inter ipsos erat. . . . eas divitias eam bonam famam magnamque nobilitatem putabant. laudis avidi, pecuniae liberales erant* [The greatest rivalry between them was for glory. . . . they thought a good name and great renown to be as wealth; greedy for praise, they were free with their money] (*Cat.* 7.6).

13. Though possible, the idea that "Ida" is the mountain in Phrygia and not a nymph seems overly difficult; see Conington 1963, *ad loc.*

14. See "Heracles, Aeneas, and Augustus" in chapter 4.

15. E.g., with Sallust's comment previously quoted in text, see Livy's preface, 9.

[I too share this desire: my heart cares nothing for life and considers that
the glory you seek to be cheaply bought even if it should cost my life.]

(A. 9.205–6)

Nisus leads as the two cut their way through the enemy camp (A. 9.320–
33), and Euryalus imitates him, no less a fighter (*nec minor Euryali caedes*,
342). Euryalus gathers spoils, and his victims and their arms, like the
victims of Homeric warriors, have impressive lineages (324–28, 360–63).
Euryalus passes all the tests, doing everything one expects of a hero; his
initiation seems complete and the mission almost succeeds: *excedunt cas-
tris et tuta capessunt* [they emerged from the enemy encampments and
headed for safety] (366).

A reflection from Euryalus' helmet betrays them to the Rutulians; Euryalus is captured, both are killed, and the mission fails. To some critics,
this peripeteia is Vergil's censure of the two heroes who, because of youth
or immoderate nature, were carried away by slaughter and greed. That
Nisus rejects, for example, none of the gifts that Iulus promises and that
he vows to the assembly that he and Euryalus will return with war
prizes—*mox hic cum spoliis ingenti caede peracta / adfore cernetis* [you will
soon see us before you with spoils won by great slaughter] (A. 9.242–43)—
have been judged proof of latent and fatal venality. Nisus and Euryalus'
killing is senseless, critics argue, an excess that causes the youths to for-
get their true purpose; Vergil condemns their moral failure (despite some
admiration for their *virtus*) and punishes them with death.[16]

While some account must be taken of the fact that Nisus halts their (or
perhaps only Euryalus') killing, *sensit enim nimia caede atque cupidine ferri*
[he felt that they were [or he was] being carried away by too much slaughter and by love of fighting] (A. 9.354), and that Euryalus' spoils cause
their capture and death, the episode need not be read as a lesson in
"good" and "bad" heroic behavior, a cautionary tale on the consequences
of *furor*.[17] Vergil nowhere lays blame on his characters; on the contrary, he
promises them eternal remembrance:

16. E.g., Otis (1963) considers that "Nisus and Euryalus are finally beaten by their bad
cupido and miss the glory that their good *cupido* envisaged" (350); similarly Quinn (1968)
observes: "the reader can hardly suppress the comment which Vergil does not
make—that those who deal out death with so little thought for their victims are perhaps
not so greatly to be pitied after all when death overtakes them too" (205). Cf. also
Schlunk 1974, 74; Lee 1980, 110–11; Duckworth 1967, 140; Anderson 1969, 79. Hardie
(1994, 26) has a sensible discussion.

17. See, for example, the comments by A. Thornton 1976, 164–72; Fitzgerald 1972,
114–37; especially Johnson 1976, chapter 3.

Fortunati ambo! si quid mea carmina possunt,
nulla dies umquam memori vos eximet aevo,
dum domus Aeneae Capitoli immobile saxum
accolet imperiumque pater Romanus habebit.

[Blessed pair! If there is any power in my verse, no passage of time will
ever deprive you of everlasting memory, so long as the household of
Aeneas will reside on the unshakable rock of the Capitol and the Roman
father will rule.]

(*A.* 9.446–49)

This promise, whatever its measures of irony or sincerity, does not seem
the sort made to those whose example instructs us how *not* to act.

Slaughtering enemies and gathering spoils are, after all, the business
of heroes, the currency of their world, the way in which *laudes* and *fama*
are won.[18] The themes and allusions that fill the episode draw our attention elsewhere—to the character of the new world in Italy, how it acts on
Nisus and Euryalus, and how it is involved in their downfall. Vergil has
created two characters who represent rather conventional cultural ideals,[19] and directs us to consider the context in which these characters and
these ideals are fatally inadequate.[20] Vergil's point lies in the texts that
loom behind the episode in *Aeneid* 9: the Homeric *Doloneia* and the fall of
Troy in the second book of the *Aeneid*.

First, we must note the surprising prominence Vergil gives the Homeric
Doloneia in the *Aeneid*.[21] It is strange that the first event of the war in Latium—after the preparatory skirmishes, the catalog of Italian troops, and
the future foretold on Aeneas' shield (Books 7 and 8)—should be a scene

18. See Lyne 1983 on the ethics of despoiling in relation to Aeneas and Pallas.

19. Wili 1930, 61: " . . . die Szene des Nisus und Euryalus . . . auch nicht als episches
Tun, sondern als ein *exemplum maiorum,* das der Dichter der Römischen Jugend
willentlich hinstellt."

20. Note that suspense plays no role in the episode; Nisus and Euryalus' failure is a
foregone conclusion, and Vergil never leaves their fates in doubt: *sed aurae / omnia
discerpunt et nubibus inrita donant* [but the winds scattered all of <Iulus' commands> and
gave them up, unheeded, to the clouds] (*A.* 9.312–13). We are reminded throughout that
all their efforts are futile: *haec rapit atque umeris nequiquam fortibus aptat* [he seized the
arms and fitted them, in vain, to his strong shoulders] (*A.* 9.364).

21. The parallels between the Homeric episode and Vergil's have been judged
instructive of Vergil's method but superficial. Heinze (1915) relegates specific
correspondences to two long footnotes (216 n. 1 and 217 n. 2) and discusses Vergil's
compression of Homeric material as a part of his more important "Neugestaltung" (217).
Knauer's (1964) discussion adds more details and ultimately reaches the same conclusion
(266–69).

modeled on *Iliad* 10. Vergil makes his own "Doloneia" the opening engagement in the Latin war, just as (no less unexpectedly) he makes the Homeric *Doloneia* the first scene in his summary of the Trojan War on Dido's mural in *Aeneid* 1 (lines 469–70). The Iliadic episode is anomalous in most respects,[22] and the problems in it are legion and well known: under cover of darkness Diomedes and Odysseus succeed by stealth and lies, killing sleeping victims and stealing, rather than winning, their horses and arms.[23] Vergil makes these acts of treachery the first association in both the Trojan War and the war in Latium; Homeric anomalies become prefatory and, as the passage continues, exemplary, the prevailing features of Euryalus' initiation.

Vergil has deliberately chosen an inappropriate backdrop for the fostering of heroic ideals, and he prepares the ground for this narrative incongruity by the assembly that precedes the mission. In the Homeric poems assemblies are rhetorical and political rather than martial duels for *kleos*, part of a dialectic about heroism in which a character's eloquence and social influence gloss his skill as a warrior.[24] Strange though *Iliad* 10 may be in other respects, the assembly is traditional, and the characters involved (except Dolon) include the greatest leaders of both sides: Agamemnon, Hector, Diomedes, and Odysseus. Vergil gives the control of his assembly to minor players, to a child and an old man: Iulus, who presides while Aeneas is away, and Aletes, *annis gravis* [burdened with years] (*A.* 9.246), who tearfully extols the resurgence of the Trojan glory of old.[25] Iulus is clearly too young for the part, *ante annos animumque gerens curamque virilem* [bearing thoughts and a man's care beyond his years] (*A.* 9.311), and it is difficult to see his role here as evidence of growing maturity and future greatness.[26] His catalog of gifts promised to Nisus owes something to Homer's but quickly grows beyond the usual

---

22. Among scholars who debate authorship and authenticity in the Homeric poems, the *Doloneia* is the section of the *Iliad* most consistently judged "spurious," and its problems have vexed even those committed to notions of the poem's unity. For bibliography and a summary of the arguments surrounding *Iliad* 10 see Heubeck 1974, 77–79 and 171.

23. On the theme of deception, see Klingner 1940; for Griffin (1986) the poet who composed the *Doloneia* "had a liking for gruesome and bizarre effects. . . . What was straightforward has become eerie" (13).

24. See Vlackos 1974, 303–62.

25. *di patrii . . . non tamen omnino Teucros delere paratis, / cum talis animos iuvenum et tam certa tulistis pectora* [Gods of the fatherland . . . despite all, you are not ready to wipe out entirely the Trojan people, when you have produced young men of such spirit and of hearts so steadfast] (*A.* 9.247–50).

26. Fowler 1919, 89–90.

gold cups, talents, and tripods, to Turnus' horse and arms, twelve captive women, and all of Latinus' private lands—extravagances commentators once blamed on Vergil's "ignorance or great exaggeration" or even tried to emend away.[27] In epic poetry, and perhaps in the *Iliad* most of all, the importance of a just apportioning of war prizes would be hard to overestimate; Vergil's catalog, however, is out of all proportion to the stakes of the mission and to the characters involved. Iulus and Aletes are disengaged from the realities of the war, a boy playacting and an old man nostalgic for the past greatness of his race. The script, so to speak, that they provide for Nisus and Euryalus has familiar lines and scenes but is oddly wrong; their naive and sentimental effusions have nothing to do with what Nisus and Euryalus find beyond the camp walls, and the drama unfolds with different rules on an unexpected stage.[28]

Vergil's other allusion in the episode, to Troy and its fall in *Aeneid* 2, continues these themes and shows their particular relevance for Euryalus' death. Turnus' insults outside the Trojan camp (*A.* 9.123–67) point to the obvious similarities between Troy and the besieged camp in Latium,[29] and Vergil strengthens this equation by repeating words and phrases in the beginning of Book 9 from his sack of Troy in Book 2.[30] The night episode itself only needs a few suggestions to advance these parallels: the Rutulians sleep after their celebrations, *somno vinoque soluti* (*A.* 9.189, 236), like the Trojans themselves on their last night, *urbem somnoque vinoque sepultam* (*A.* 2.265). Vergil equates Aeneas' loss of Creusa in the ruins of the city (*A.* 2.737–55) with Nisus' separation from Euryalus in the dark woods (*A.* 9.384–93).[31]

No less than the Homeric *Doloneia*, the fall of Troy in the *Aeneid* is a series of deceptions in an unrecognizable heroic world, with *dolus* (treacherous cunning) as its pervasive theme and darkness as its medium.[32] Where traditional heroes seek glory or an honorable death (like

27. Conington 1963, *ad A.* 9.265; see McLoughlin 1968 for a summary of views.

28. Compare Evander's reminiscing as he sends Pallas into battle; see "Loss and the Domestic World" in chapter 3.

29. The camp itself is called *Troia* (*A.* 10.378); Turnus compares himself to Menelaus (*A.* 9.137–40), Lavinia to Helen (*coniuge praerepta, A.* 9.137), and the Trojan deceits of the present to those of the past (*A.* 9.150–55).

30. E.g., *A.* 2.291 and 9.135, *A.* 2.624–25 and 9.144–45, *A.* 2.198 and 9.148, *A.* 2.165–67 and 9.150–52, *A.* 2.401 and 9.152. See Conington 1963, *ad loc.*, and Moskalew 1982, 229–31, for these and other parallels; cf. Putnam 1965, 49–50.

31. See "Troy and Childhood" in this chapter.

32. *Dolus* appears in Book 2 eight times out of twenty-six total occurrences in the *Aeneid*, twice its frequency in any other book in the poem; Vergil uses it four times in Book 4 and four times in Book 1 (three times of Cupid's deception).

Sallust's early Roman *iuvenes*),[33] we instead meet the code of the new hero in Sinon, a Greek, *paratus / seu versare dolos seu certae occumbere morti* [ready either to make his deception work or to face certain death] (*A.* 2.61–62), and in Coroebus, an ally of Troy, who by a comparable travesty wonders, *dolus an virtus, quis in hoste requirat?* [trickery or valor, who asks in the midst of the enemy?] (*A.* 2.390). At the end of Book 1 Dido asks Aeneas for a conventional narrative of the fall of Troy, the arms and the men:

> multa super Priamo rogitans, super Hectore multa;
> nunc quibus Aurorae venisset filius armis,
> nunc quales Diomedis equi, nunc quantus Achilles.

[She asked many times about Priam, many times about Hector; now with what arms the son of Dawn had come, now what sort were the horses of Diomedes, now how tall Achilles stood.]

(A. 1.750–52)

For Aeneas heroic grandeur—weaponry, stature, and ancestry—is a meaningless anachronism and he characterizes the final night of Troy in terms appropriate to the new world:

> talibus insidiis periurique arte Sinonis
> credita res, captique dolis lacrimisque coactis
> quos neque Tydides nec Larisaeus Achilles,
> non anni domuere decem, non mille carinae.

[By such plots and the cunning of the liar, Sinon, the tale was believed, and we were captured by treachery and false tears—we whom neither Diomedes nor Larisaean Achilles had defeated, nor ten years, nor a thousand ships.]

(A. 2.195–98)

This statement is both irony and a simple definition: the war begins with Paris' deception and ends with a complex of others—*insidiae, doli, periuri ars.*

By importing these associations into his night episode in Book 9 Vergil asserts that the fall of old Troy pervades and characterizes "new" Troy as well: Vergil clusters words for betrayal and deception—*fallax, fallere, insidiae, furtum, fraus, prodere*—to mark this reenactment.[34] Under Nisus' tu-

---

33. See Sallust *Cat.* 7; cf. also Pallas' prayer before his fight with Turnus (*A.* 10.460–63).

34. In the 326 lines of the episode (*A.* 9.176–502) these words occur as least as often as in any other whole book of the *Aeneid* except Books 4 (not surprisingly), 6, and 10. *Dolus* is never used in Vergil's night episode, perhaps to avoid the too-obvious etymology, *dolus* < Δόλων.

telage Euryalus' killing and despoiling quickly escalate, and he presses on, inflamed with his cunning, *hic furto fervidus instat* (A. 9.350).[35] The darkness that at first conceals him becomes a trap that leads to his capture, and he is finally caught, overwhelmed by the deceptiveness of the terrain and of night, *fraude loci et noctis . . . oppressum* (A. 9.396–98). Euryalus wears the arms he has taken (A. 9.365–66), but the spoils that should be a token of his success betray him (373–74) and block his escape (384–85). Light is inimical to Nisus and Euryalus, *lux inimica propinquat* (A. 9.355), and their element is shadow—variations on the phrase *noctis per umbram* become a refrain that marks their way through the enemy camp (A. 9.314, 373, 411).

The darkness and treachery particularly associated with Troy and with the Homeric *Doloneia* have become generalized in Vergil's Latium, so much so that they affect both sides in the conflict indifferently: the Trojans, victims of Greek trickery in *Aeneid* 2, are its perpetrators in Book 9, and Nisus and Euryalus are cast as Homer's Odysseus and Diomedes. This generalizing should guide our judgment of Nisus and Euryalus and prevent our simplifying the implications of their actions and deaths.

A further parallel from the fall of Troy in Book 2 helps put the episode in its proper light. Coroebus urges the Trojans to trick the Danaans by wearing Greek arms to infiltrate the enemy ranks. They succeed at first, until Coroebus is driven mad (*insano amore*, A. 2.343) by the sight of his betrothed, Cassandra, in chains; he dies in a love suicide, trying to free her from her Greek captors. There are correspondences between Coroebus' story and the story of Nisus and Euryalus (as well as suggestions of Aeneas and Creusa and of Orpheus and Eurydice, to which I return later in this chapter), but for the present argument we need only note that while Coroebus' stratagem is far from conventionally heroic, nothing in the text invites or even allows censure.[36] All his fellow Trojans agree to his plan, including Aeneas and Rhipeus, the "most just man who lived in Troy,"[37] and Aeneas tells the story in Carthage without apology, only

---

35. *Furto* goes more naturally with *fervidus*, as Servius and Donatus take it (*ad loc.*), and not with *instat* (so Conington 1963, *ad loc.*).

36. Heinze (1915, 37–38) and Conington (1963, *ad A.* 2.341) note that Vergil had secure precedent for making Coroebus a model of rashness and stupidity and still did not: Servius (*ad A.* 2.341) cites Euphorion, whose Coroebus is a fool (*stultus*), a quality amplified by later writers: in Zenobius he stands on the shore counting waves.

37. *Ripheus, iustissimus unus / qui fuit in Teucris et servantissimus aequi* (A. 2.426–27). Aeneas himself seems not to have worn Greek arms; see Heinze 1915, 36–39.

regret and horror that the plan did not succeed. Coroebus is not a character study of a failed personality; his strategy is of a piece with the larger context of the fall of the city (insidiae, doli, periuri ars).

By the strength of Vergil's allusions the ethos of Troy provides the same context for the events in Book 9. It must be granted that Nisus and Euryalus' killing is excessive, that Euryalus' spoils are a fatal immoderation, and that Nisus' attempted rescue seems a lover's madness. The real question, however, is not whether Nisus and Euryalus are right or wrong in acting as they do but whether or not their behavior is inevitable: their actions are above all repetitions, familiar shapes emerging in a landscape formed in the likeness of Vergil's Troy.

TROY AND CHILDHOOD

Darkness and the labyrinthine woods are a refuge through which Nisus escapes and even returns again to search for Euryalus, *perplexum iter omne revolvens / fallacis silvae* [unraveling again the whole twisted path of the treacherous wood] (*A.* 9.391–92); in contrast, Euryalus, the child, is lost and helpless. The deaths of child characters recur throughout Vergil's narrative of the fall of Troy as well, put constantly before our eyes by modifications of traditional stories or allusions to obscure ones. The first Trojan to urge that the horse be brought into the city is Thymoetes, acting either as an agent of fate or as a traitor, in retaliation for Priam's killing of his infant son (*A.* 2.34).[38] Though the death of Laocoon's son (or sons) is a traditional part of the Trojan legend, Vergil alone of the many extant sources makes them children: *et primum parva duorum / corpora natorum serpens amplexus* [the snake first entwined the small bodies of the two sons] (*A.* 2.213–14).[39] We can further compare Panthus, the priest of Apollo who flees the citadel with the city's gods and his young son (*sacra manu victosque deos parvumque nepotem / ipse trahit, A.* 2.320–21); in the *Iliad* Panthus' son is a grown warrior who is almost killed in battle but is spared at the last moment by Apollo.[40]

---

38. Servius (*ad loc.*) attributes this story to Euphorion: a prophecy declares that a son born in Troy on a particular day is fated to bring ruin on the city. When on that day sons are born to both Thymoetes and Priam, the son of Thymoetes is killed while Paris is spared.

39. Austin 1964, 94–99 and 105–6.

40. *Il.* 15.521–22; see Heinze (1915) 33–35.

The deaths of children become a more general threat to families and households as the episode progresses. Neoptolemus' attack (*A.* 2.469–558) destroys both a kingdom and a family: the women of Priam's household embrace and kiss the palace columns for the last time (*A.* 2.490), and the fifty chambers of Priam's sons fall in ruins, *spes tanta nepotum* [so great a hope of offspring] (*A.* 2.503–5).[41] Polites is killed before his parents' eyes (*ante oculos . . . et ora parentum, A.* 2.531), and Priam dies at the family altar in the blood of his son (*A.* 2.550–58). The threat to Aeneas' household forms the final third of the episode (*A.* 2.650–795): he starts the book as hero and defender of the city, and he ends as son, father, and husband.[42]

I will return at the end of this chapter to the disappearance of Creusa, the last "betrayal" of the episode; I would now like to consider one further passage that shows Vergil's persistent association of Troy with the end of childhood and the loss of innocence, this time not from Book 2, but from Vergil's pictorial summary of the fall of the city in the first book.

The retrospective of the Trojan War in Dido's mural (*A.* 1.455–93) anticipates and confirms the themes made explicit in Books 2 and 9. The *Doloneia* is depicted first, followed by the first death of a "child" in the *Aeneid*, Troilus, *infelix puer atque impar congressus Achilli* [Troilus, unfortunate boy and no match in battle for Achilles] (475). Though Troilus' place among the "fates of Ilium" explains his prominence on the mural,[43] Vergil nowhere alludes to his role in the fall of the city; all the details in the passage (the longest of all the scenes Vergil describes) emphasize the way he dies, an unarmed boy, *armis amissis*, against the greatest of the Achaians. Vergil intends to recall other associations. By Hellenistic times Troilus had become a byword for parents' grief at their children's death, μεῖον ἐδάκρυσεν Τρωΐλος ἢ Πρίαμος [Troilus wept less than Priam] (Callimachus frag. 491 Pfeiffer), and he remained so into Roman times: Cicero quotes Callimachus approvingly, and Horace's *Odes* 2.9.16 depends on the familiarity of the saying: *nec impubem parentes / Troilon aut Phrygiae sorores / flevere semper* [not even his parents or Phrygian sisters wept always for young Troilus].[44]

---

41. See *"spes gregis"* in chapter 1.

42. Klingner 1967, 414–15.

43. Troy would not fall if Troilus lived to his twentieth birthday. Plautus (*Bacchides* 953) gives three "fates of Troy": the death of Troilus, the theft of the Palladium, and the wooden horse passing through the Phrygian gates; see Austin 1971, *ad loc.,* for bibliography and discussion. Troilus receives only brief mention in the *Iliad* as one of the many sons Priam has lost (*Il.* 24.257).

44. Cicero *Tusc.* 1.93: *non male ait Callimachus multo saepius lacrimasse Priamum quam*

The proverbial suggestions of Troilus—the helplessness, pain, and sadness at a child's untimely death—prepare the way for the panel that follows, the center of the mural, its most important section. The Trojan women offer a peplos to appease Athena:

> interea ad templum non aequae Palladis ibant
> crinibus Iliades passis peplumque ferebant
> suppliciter, tristes et tunsae pectora palmis.

[Meanwhile the Trojan women, with hair unbound, were processing to the temple of hostile Pallas; they bore a peplos in supplication and, grieving, beat their breasts with their hands.]

(A. 1.479–81)

It has been suggested that Vergil's brief and "at first sight disappointing" centerpiece alludes both to the corresponding scene at *Iliad* 6.263–311 and to a procession in Calvus' *Io*,[45] a procession that appears as an elaborate (and awkward) conceit in the proem of the *Ciris* (21–53).[46] In Calvus, Athena's festival provides a stage for the real drama at hand: the lust of Jupiter, the wrath of Juno, Io's metamorphosis, and her torment by the gadfly. Io is a child (it seems),[47] playing with a ball during the procession, and in opening her cloak for easier play she catches Jupiter's eye, *prodita ludo* (*Ciris*, 150).[48] If this suggestion is correct, at the heart of his summary of the Trojan War Vergil puts what is a minor event in the *Iliad* but the critical moment in the *Io*, the child at play as she falls victim to adulthood and sexuality. We recognize in Io the same transition and the same loss as in the *virgo* of Catullus 65 or in Ariadne in 64. Vergil suggests an analogy between Troy and adulthood, between the Trojan War and the end of innocence.

To impute these themes and to attribute such allusive weight to Calvus' *Io*, a work almost entirely lost, is admittedly speculative.[49] We may fur-

---

Troilum. [Callimachus is right when he says, "Priam wept more often by far than Troilus"]; Pfeiffer *(ad loc.)* cites these and further references.

45. See Thomas 1987 for the importance of the central images in ecphrases and the significance and provenance of this one.

46. First proposed by Sudhaus; see Lyne 1970, 154–55.

47. The following reconstruction of the *Io* is in Lyne 1970, 45 and 154–55.

48. See Lyne 1970, *ad loc.*, for context and sense; Vergil may echo Calvus (*prodita ludo, Ciris* 150) in the death of Rhesus (*prodita somno, A.* 1.470).

49. Io is also depicted or suggested in the most important moments of the *Aeneid*, in images, moreover, that have stoutly resisted explication (and would presumably be clearer if the *Io* were extant): Turnus goes into battle bearing a shield embossed with a picture of Io, and the *balteus* that Turnus strips from Pallas—the controlling image of the

ther compare, however, Vergil's other pictorial display, the sculpted doors on the temple at Cumae that greet the Trojans when they land in Italy (*A.* 6.20–33). The panels offer an even more explicit depiction of lost children and lost posterity (Androgeos, the sons of the Athenians, and Icarus) as well as themes of childhood innocence and monstrous love (Ariadne and Pasiphae).[50] The Carthaginian mural of the Trojan War depicts the stock and stem of this lost posterity; Vergil, by including responding images on the doors in Book 6, implies that the old stock, engrafted in Latium, will take hold and produce the same effects in the new world as well.

DIDO

In the narrative of the Trojans' wandering after they leave Carthage, Dido's gifts are a leitmotif. They appear only three times, always connected to child characters and always in stock epic scenes: to Iulus in the games in Book 5, to Pallas in his funeral scene in Book 11, and to Iulus again in the assembly before the night mission.[51] In Book 9 they connect the fall of Troy and Euryalus' death with a larger complex of ideas:

> bina dabo argento perfecta atque aspera signis
> pocula, devicta genitor quae cepit Arisba,
> et tripodas geminos, auri duo magna talenta,
> cratera antiquum quem dat Sidonia Dido.

---

final scene in the poem—is decorated with Io's descendants, the daughters of Danaus. For Io, see Ross 1987, 157–63, and O'Hara 1990, 78–81; for the Danaids, see "The Daughters of Danaus" in chapter 4.

50. Though we might have expected twin doors to have an even distribution of lines, Vergil's passage is notably asymmetrical: three lines for one door (lines 20–22) and seven and a half lines for the other (lines 23–30). This physical asymmetry, however, gives special emphasis to the themes of the relief, arranged by Vergil into (nearly) precise symmetrical blocks. An opening section of three lines describes the deaths of sons (of Androgeos and the Athenian youths sent as tribute to Minos), and a final section, also of three lines, describes the death of another son, Icarus, an image *not* represented on the doors (lines 30–33). Embedded within this frame Vergil sets an eight-line diptych: four lines describe Pasiphae, driven mad by Poseidon and mated with a bull; the next three and a half describe the great love of Ariadne and the rescue of Theseus. This passage has received particularly good treatments by Segal (1966), who connects Icarus with Marcellus (50–52), and by Putnam (1987).

51. Iulus' horse in the *lusus Troiae* is a gift from Dido (*A.* 5.570–72) and Pallas is buried in cloaks she has woven (*A.* 11.73–75) and given as gifts to Aeneas (*A.* 11.75 = *A.* 4.264). See "The Death of Pallas" in chapter 4.

[I will give you twin cups, worked in silver and heavily engraved, which my father won when he sacked Arisba, and two tripods, two great talents of gold, and an ancient crater, a gift from Sidonian Dido.]

(A. 9.263–66)

Tripods, talents of gold, and silver cups prove a hero's *virtus* and are record of his deeds; the crater given to Aeneas by Dido recalls instead her death and Aeneas' abandonment of her. Her gifts, here and throughout the *Aeneid,* break through the order and comprehensibility implied by familiar heroic acts and call to mind how tortuous and how lacking in clarity the issues of Vergil's poem are. Aeneas in Carthage is a man lost between love and the constraints of life and fate. Between Dido and Italy there is no simple or "right" course for him to take: Vergil's world demands that Aeneas betray her, without consolation and without any resolution of his guilt. Dido's is an insistent, alternative voice in the poem, rebutting the simple claims of heroism that Iulus here attempts to imitate and that Euryalus anticipates.

Vergil uses this allusion to Dido as a preface to Euryalus' initiation, and he concludes the episode with others. Euryalus' mother and Dido greet the same dawn: *et iam prima novo spargebat lumine terras / Tithoni croceum linquens Aurora cubile* [Aurora leaves the saffron bed of Tithonus and flecks the earth with her first light] (A. 4.584–85 = A. 9.459–60); Vergil elsewhere repeats whole or partial lines from dawn formulae, but nowhere else does he repeat two lines in their entirety.[52] Both women, furthermore, look from battlements on the ruins of their lives and loves: one on the head of Euryalus carried by on a pike and the other on the Trojan fleet sailing from Carthage. Euryalus' leaving is felt as a desertion:[53]

> tune ille senectae
> sera meae requies, potuisti linquere solam,
> crudelis?

[Were you able to leave me, cruel one, alone as I am, my comfort in old age, late though it came?]

(A. 9.481–83)

Crudelis, placed last in the sentence in enjambment, occurs in the *Aeneid*

---

52. E.g., A. 3.589 = A. 4.7; see Moskalew 1982, 66. It might be significant that the second line, *Tithoni croceum linquens Aurora cubile,* is borrowed from the weather signs of the first *Georgic* (447), portending hail that will destroy the vines just as the grapes become ripe (*mitis . . . uvas*).

53. Compare Aeneas' lament for Anchises: *hic me, pater optime, fessum / deseris* [At this point do you desert me, best of fathers, weary as I am?] (A. 3.710–11).

only here and in Book 4,[54] where Dido complains to Aeneas about his se-
cret preparations for departure:

> quin etiam hiberno moliris sidere classem
> et mediis properas Aquilonibus ire per altum,
> crudelis?

[Are you preparing your fleet to sail even in time of winter? Do you
rush, cruel one, though facing northern storms, to cross the sea?]
(A. 4.309–11)

ADULTHOOD AND *AMOR*

Vergil's parallels between Dido and Euryalus' mother, or between Nisus
and Euryalus and Coroebus and Cassandra, are not obvious ones to make
and should even strike us as bizarre. The relationships involved—familial, Platonic, and erotic love—are of markedly different character, and we
should not let our familiarity with the poem deaden the surprise of Vergil's analogies. Vergil has taken pains to give these very different losses
an unmistakable sameness, employing reminiscences of vocabulary or
locale, until each love partially reenacts other loves, and all suffer the
same end. By an equally unexpected analogy, Vergil connects Nisus' attempt to rescue Euryalus with Orpheus' journey to the underworld to
bring back Eurydice (G. 4.453–527) and with Aeneas' return to Troy for
Creusa (A. 2.735–95).[55] I would like to discuss two different effects of
these parallels, first (and only briefly) in connection to Nisus' death, to
examine the means by which these analogies are made.

When Euryalus becomes lost in the dark woods Vergil tells the story
of his capture and death from Nisus' point of view. This is an important
change and gives the failed initiation and the deceptions of the epic
world a new focus, the loss of a loved one, another of the poem's great
themes and linked, as well, with darkness.[56] The eagerness for glory and
praise that spurs Nisus on at the start of the mission now becomes *amor*:
Vergil underlines this change by describing Nisus' love suicide with the
conceits and vocabulary of conventional heroism.

Nisus despairs at Euryalus' capture and resolves to free him or to die
in the attempt:

54. Conington 1963, *ad A.* 9.483.
55. Putnam 1965, 41–63.
56. E.g., Eurydice in the underworld and Creusa in Troy.

> quid faciat? qua vi iuvenem, quibus audeat armis
> eripere? an sese medios moriturus in enses
> inferat et pulchram properet per vulnera mortem.

[What could he do? By what force of arms might he dare to tear free the young man? Or should he plunge, prepared to die, in the thick of the enemy and rush to a noble death through wounds?]

(A. 9.399–401)

Lines 400–401 are formulae used to describe the *aristeiai* of heroes. Vergil's bees in the fourth *Georgic* are characterized by ethnographical and heroic *topoi*,[57] and they give their lives for their king "seeking a noble death through wounds," *pulchramque petunt per vulnera mortem* (G. 4.218); in the *Aeneid* the Trojans and the Rutulians fight by the same inspiration (cf. G. 4.218 and A. 11.647). The insertion of the future participle *moriturus* between the adjective and prepositional phrase (*medios . . . in enses*) is equally formulaic: Priam's arming scene on the final night of Troy is a pathetic imitation of the conceit, as is his futile attempt to resist Neoptolemus and the Greek assault: *ac densos fertur moriturus in hostis* [he made for the thronged enemy, prepared to die] (A. 2.511). In Book 9 Helenor stands against the Latin armies, trapped alone outside the Trojan battlements, and prefers a hero's death to flight: *iuvenis medios moriturus in hostis / irruit et qua tela videt densissima tendit* [the man rushed headlong into the thronged enemy, prepared to die, and aimed for the place where he saw the missiles fall thickest] (A. 9.554–55).[58] In the present passage Vergil gives this vocabulary a different valence: heroic *topoi* become an expression of Nisus' love.

Heroic *topoi* are most strikingly transformed in the scene of Nisus' death. At the beginning of the episode he complains about inactivity and longs to win glory:

> aut pugnam aut aliquid iamdudum invadere magnum
> mens agitat mihi, nec placida contenta quiete est.

---

57. See Thomas 1982b, 70–92, and Griffin 1979, 61–80.

58. Cf. A. 11.741, *in medios moriturus et ipse* of Tarchon's charge, an overtly Homeric passage that Knauer (1964, 424) compares to *Il.* 4.338–48; cf. also Coroebus, *et sese medium iniecit periturus in agmen* (A. 2.408) and the future indicative of Aeneas' grandiloquent *numquam omnes hodie moriemur inulti* (A. 2.670); see "The Epic World and Rome" in chapter 1.

[My heart now urges me to do battle or to attempt some great deed, and
it can not abide untroubled peace.]

(*A.* 9.186–87)

Line 186 is in the idiom we expect (Conington compares *Il.* 10.220, 319);
heroes are made restless by *placida quies,* the conventional antithesis to
deeds and warfare.[59] The heroic lines that open the episode are balanced
by responding lines with repeated vocabulary at the end:

> tum super exanimum sese proiecit amicum
> confossus, placidaque ibi demum morte quievit.

[Then pierced through, he threw himself on his lifeless friend, and there
at last found quiet in the peace of death.]

(*A.* 9.444–45)

The dissolution of heroism is summarized by these two passages that
frame the episode. Instead of a hero's *fama* and *gloria* for deeds nobly
done, love overwhelms Nisus, and he finds death (*placida . . . morte
quievit*), the only real respite the poem can offer. In Vergil's poetry, implicitly, *amor* is neither a refuge from nor an alternative to the epic world,
but a fatal vulnerability.

Placida and *quies* are significant words in the *Aeneid. Quies* (often with
placida) consistently forebodes treachery or simply means death. Palinurus is soothed to sleep (*placida laxabant membra quiete, A.* 5.836) before he
is thrown overboard. *Prima quies mortalibus aegris* describes the deceiving
calm before the Danaans leave the horse on Troy's last night (*A.* 2.268),
and in Turnus' sleep, *mediam nigra carpebat nocte quietem* (*A.* 7.414), Allecto
appears. *Quies* is a synonym for death in phrases like *dura quies* (*A.* 12.309
= 10.745; cf. *A.* 6.371, 7.598, etc.). Respite in the conventional heroic world
is peace and freedom from *labor;* for Vergil this is an impossibility, and
in his epic the only real peace is death itself: Palinurus begs Aeneas to
transport him across the Styx, *sedibus ut saltem placidis in morte quiescam*
(*A.* 6.371).[60] *Placida, quies,* and these associations converge in Deiphobus'
betrayal by Helen on the night Troy falls:

59. It is equally common in erotic contexts: Varro Atacinus, *Argo.* frag. 8, *omnia noctis
erant placida composta quiete* (the sleeplessness of love-tormented Medea = Ap. Rh. *Argo.*
3.749–50); and probably in the *Zmyrna* (see Lyne 1970, 43). Cf. generally Wlosok 1967,
37–38 and 142; Pease (1935, *ad A.* 4.5) gives later uses.

60. Equally telling, when these words do not forebode trouble they often occur in
passages that describe literary or scientific fictions: the Italian landscape (*secura quies et
nescia fallere vita* of the *laus vitae rusticae, G.* 2.467), and the marvelous Hesiodic spring (*ver
illud erat*), an untroubled respite between the hot and cold extremes of winter and

tum me confectum curis somnoque gravatum
infelix habuit thalamus, pressitque iacentem
dulcis et alta quies placidaeque simillima morti.

[Then the bedchamber, fateful and barren, held me worn with care and
heavy with sleep; rest, soothing and deep, most like still death, pressed
upon me as I lay.]

(*A.* 6.520–22)

THE DEATH OF EURYALUS

Catullus' preoccupation with faithlessness and suffering pervades much
of his poetry. Remote times and characters (the age of heroes in Catullus
64), the conventions of genre (in the epithalamia), and even translation,
do not preclude the abiding issues of "subjective" poetry; to the contrary,
they offer new vehicles for old injuries. Catullus asserts that the failings
of his private world are universal and timeless, that there is no "then"
and "now," no heroic past and degenerate present, only a steady contin-
uum of loss and pain.

The losses and pain of Vergil's poetry are timeless in the same way.
Euryalus is not simply another (especially pathetic) casualty of war
whose death can be felt from a comfortable distance in a narrative about
a remote time and place. Because he figuratively leaves childhood and
enters adulthood, his initiation implies natural growth, a universal and
inevitable process. Childhood is a transient state of security and love,
and the deceptions that cause him to fail are the intractable realities of
adulthood. Vergil's preoccupation with such "reality" is clear in his de-

---

summer (*si non tanta quies iret frigusque caloremque, G.* 2.344); see Ross 1987, 109–28. The
golden age, not surprisingly, is called *placida pax* (*A.* 8.325).

For an impressive use of *quies* (perhaps inspired by Vergil's variations) compare Lucan
de Bello Civili 1.236–61: warfare and peace are opposed at the beginning of the passage, as
the noise and clash of Caesar's battle horns disturb the quiet of the countryside and rouse
the people from their beds (*rupta quies populi,* 239). Civil war, an unnatural event, creates
unnatural reversals: by the end of the passage *quies* has changed character to become not
warfare's antithesis but its condition:

sed quantum, volucres cum bruma coercet,
rura silent, mediusque tacet sine murmure pontus,
tanta quies.

[Such was the silence, even as fields are still when winter's chill drives birds to
silent roost, as the sea far from land, in dead calm, is without murmur.]

(1.259–61)

scription of Euryalus' death and in the passages that depict Orpheus' loss of Eurydice and Aeneas' loss of Creusa.

Orpheus' loss of Eurydice is Vergil's paradigm of human limitations. The archetypal poet of science who can control nature and even the power of death is nevertheless subject to the irrationality of *furor* and the typical constraints of the world at large: *omnia vincit Amor.*[61] This paradigm is expressed in primary colors: darkness is the underworld itself; Orpheus' love is all-consuming and his grief is inconsolable and fatal. Despite the paradigmatic treatment of loss and love, Orpheus never becomes a "symbol" or an abstraction, and Vergil describes his grief with a plainness that approaches banality:

> qualis populea maerens philomela sub umbra
> amissos queritur fetus, quos durus arator
> observans nido implumis detraxit; et illa
> flet noctem, ramoque sedens miserabile carmen
> integrat, et maestis late loca questibus implet.

[[Orpheus grieves] . . . just as the nightingale grieving in the shade of the poplar laments the loss of her still-unfeathered young—the young lost when the fierce plowman found them and stole them from the nest; she weeps the night through and, sitting on a branch, renews her pitiable song, filling the wood with sorrowful cries.]

(*G.* 4.511–15)

Conington, *ad loc.,* compares *Odyssey* 16.216–18 and 19.518–23, and though Homer's similes—the farmer's robbery of a vulture's nest and the *aetion* of the nightingale's song—share some details with Vergil's, there is more here than a simple blending of canonical models. Homer's second passage shows the effect that Vergil has avoided:[62]

> ὡς δ' ὅτε Πανδαρέου κούρη, χλωρηὶς ἀηδών,
> καλὸν ἀείδῃσιν ἔαρος νέον ἱσταμένοιο,
> δενδρέων ἐν πετάλοισι καθεζομένη πυκινοῖσιν,
> ἥ τε θαμὰ τρωπῶσα χέει πολυηχέα φωνήν,
> παῖδ' ὀλοφυρομένη Ἴτυλον φίλον, ὅν ποτε χαλκῷ

---

61. See Ross 1975, 105.

62. *Od.* 16.216–18: κλαῖον δὲ λιγέως, ἀδινώτερον ἤ τ' οἰωνοί, / φῆναι ἢ αἰγυπιοὶ γαμψώνυχες, οἷσί τε τέκνα / ἀγρόται ἐξείλοντο πάρος πετεηνὰ γενέσθαι [They wept aloud, more even than birds lament, eagles or taloned vultures, whose young the farmers steal before they have come to full feather]. Vergil does not simply imitate the "naturalism" of Homer's farmers and vultures; his simile deliberately alludes to Philomela to create the contrast between mythic deaths and those of life-size characters.

κτεῖνε δι' ἀφραδίας, κοῦρον Ζήθοιο ἄνακτος,
ὣς καὶ ἐμοὶ δίχα θυμὸς ὀρώρεται ἔνθα καὶ ἔνθα

[As when the pale nightingale, the daughter of Pandareos, makes beautiful song when spring has just arrived—sitting among the trees' dense leaves she pours forth her echoing song, modulating with changing notes, lamenting her dear son Itylus, the son of lord Zethos, whom long ago in her madness she murdered with a sword—even so my heart tossed forward and back in doubt.]

(*Od.* 19.518–24)

Vergil refashions a mythical exemplum, Philomela's lament for her son Itylus, into an everyday rural event. We are not, as we expect, asked to experience Orpheus' loss through a monumental paradigm of lost progeny from fable; we are surprised, instead, to find the myth (Philomela) transformed into a present-day manifestation of mourning and loss (the *philomela*), reenacted according to real-life violence and innocence, the *durus arator* and the *fetus implumis*.[63]

An earlier passage in the *Georgics,* rather than the vulture simile from *Iliad* 16, provides the context for the present one. Vergil describes the fecundity of Italian soil:

> non ullo ex aequore cernes
> plura domum tardis decedere plaustra iuvencis;
> aut unde iratus silvam devexit arator
> et nemora evertit multos ignava per annos,
> antiquasque domus avium cum stirpibus imis
> eruit; illae altum nidis petiere relictis.

[You will not see from any other land more carts drive home, their oxen weary and slow; nor any other place from where the wrathful plowman has carried off the stands of trees and cut down the groves, unproductive for many years, and has dug out, deep roots and all, the ancient homes of birds; the birds seek the sky, their nests abandoned.]

(*G.* 2.205–10)

The farmer returns home enriched; the birds are driven from their homes. Success (*plura . . . plaustra*), demands an assault on nature and on innocence (*nemora . . . multos ignava per annos / . . . domus avium*). Farming, like civilization itself, is a constant war against nature and the power of growth, and farmers require violence and destruction for survival.[64] Or-

---

63. Mynors (1990, *ad G.* 4.511) calls Vergil's simile "a piece of unreasoning cruelty."
64. On this see Thomas 1988a and 1988b, *ad G.* 2.205 and pp. 23–24. For farming as

pheus' loss, by its comparison to the ("real") nightingale's, is not particular or unique, but another of the recurring losses that everyday life demands.

Aeneas' failure to save Creusa in Book 2 recalls the loss of Eurydice,[65] and Vergil's allusions remind us that in early accounts of the Trojan War Creusa was called Eurydice.[66] In the *Aeneid* the conventional lamentation of the stricken lover and the prolonged and wandering death that characterize the suffering of Orpheus (like Gallus' suffering in the tenth *Eclogue*) are gone. Aeneas' parting from Creusa is brief:

> haec ubi dicta dedit, lacrimantem et multa volentem
> dicere deseruit, tenuisque recessit in auras.
> ter conatus ibi collo dare bracchia circum;
> ter frustra comprensa manus effugit imago,
> par levibus ventis volucrique simillima somno.
> sic demum socios consumpta nocte reviso.

[With these words she left me, though I wept and wished to say more; she faded away into the gentle breeze. Three times I tried to put my arms about her neck; three times her shade, embraced in vain, fled my hands, as if a soft wind, most like swift sleep. Then at last, with the night waning, I rejoined my companions.]

(*A.* 2.790–95)

Sic demum tells the whole story and is, as Austin says, "the abyss of sorrow."[67] As in the *philomela* simile, here, too, Vergil breaks through the conventions of loss and suffering by introducing, almost imperceptibly, present-day reality, this time by an allusion to Catullus. The burning of Troy, the slaughter of his men by Greeks and by fellow Trojans, and the death

---

warfare see *G.* 2.279–83 and 3.346–48 (two of many possible examples) with Thomas 1988b, *ad loc.*, and Ross 1987, 32–94 and 128–48. Birds (like trees) are frequent victims of civilization: even Vergil's description of the dead dove in Anchises' funeral game (*A.* 5.517–18) is notably sympathetic. They fare better in the precivilized world, in primitive Latium along the banks of the Tiber (*A.* 7.30–34), and in Evander's kingdom (*A.* 8.455–56).

The destruction of trees in the *Georgics* is constant, except for the oleaster, which is strong enough to survive all human interventions and even fire (*G.* 2.303–14); the same tree, nevertheless, meets its match in the *Aeneid* (*foliis oleaster amaris, G.* 2.314 = *A.* 12.766): the Trojans kill it, rooting it out to clear the field for battle.

65. Heurgon 1931; cf. Putnam 1965, 41–48.

66. She is Eurydice in the *Cypria* and *Ilias Parva*, according to Paus. 10.26.1, and in Ennius frag. 36 Skutsch. Aeneas' wife is first called Creusa in Augustan times: see Heinze 1915, 57–63.

67. Austin 1964, *ad A.* 2.795. Vergil repeats lines 790–91 from Orpheus' loss of Eurydice in the fourth *Georgic*.

of Priam are all part of a general tragedy in which Creusa's disappearance is climactic. Aeneas professes the depth of his grief in a single sentence:

> quem non incusavi amens hominumque deorumque
> aut quid in eversa vidi crudelius urbe?

[Whom did I not blame of both men and gods as I raved or what deed more cruel did witness in the fall of the city?]

(A. 2.745–46)

At such a climax it would be remarkable if Vergil had produced these words "unconsciously," indifferent to or careless about their ability to recall other lines in other poems. The interrogative *quid . . . crudelius urbe* is repeated from Catullus' lament in poem 62 for the "violent" separation and the lost innocence that accompany marriage and the beginning of adult love:[68]

> Hespere, quis caelo fertur crudelior ignis?
> qui natam possis complexu avellere matris,
> complexu matris retinentem avellere natam,
> et iuveni ardenti castam donare puellam.
> quid faciunt hostes capta crudelius urbe?

[Hesperus, what light crossing the sky seems more cruel? You tear away the daughter from the mother's embrace, the daughter, even as she clings, from the embrace of the mother, and give the chaste maiden to the burning youth. What more cruel wrong does the enemy commit when a city is taken?]

(62.20–24)

The "cruel" *raptus* of the young bride is an obvious conceit in a highly mannered poem.[69] To deny that Vergil's is a deliberate allusion on the grounds that the Catullan context is playful and mannered or to assert that Vergil's use of the phrase is deliberate but a "striking reversal of meaning"[70] misses the point: Catullus persistently involves his own preoccupations in his poetry, even in poems that seem only to be literary exercises (e.g., 66).[71] The emphatically repeated *matris* and *natam* (lines

---

68. Austin (1964, *ad A.* 2.746) is undecided about this connection; Conington (1963, *ad loc.*) cites the Catullan line without comment. Most accept Vergil's line as an adaptation: Westendorp-Boerma (1958) considers it a certain imitation but "a conscious inversion" (59); so Wigodsky 1972, 127, and Commager 1983, 24 n. 14.

69. Fedeli 1981.

70. Wigodsky 1972, 127.

71. Clausen 1970, 90–92, and chapter 2 of this book.

21–22) with elaborate chiasmus,[72] the second *natam* strengthened by *retinentem*, go beyond the simpler repetitions of the poem[73] and its traditional figures; here these features stress, beneath the mannered surface, mother, daughter, and their separation. Marriage is the experience of Ariadne: the end of innocence and trust, the dissolution of the family,[74] and the beginning of the uncertainties and faithlessness that Catullus finds endemic in his world. Surely it would be more surprising if Catullus' epithalamia were exempt from the bitterness at change and decline that dominates so much of his work.

Vergil recognizes the traces of bitterness that play at the edges of the marriage poems; this bitterness is Catullus' hallmark and the sense that Aeneas' loss of Creusa is meant to evoke.[75] Like the *casta puella*, Aeneas is violently torn from his home and his past, and he must leave, by the terms of the allusion, a figurative childhood of security, trust, and love. Vergil equates the world that Aeneas must now enter with Catullus' (adult) world of infidelities and discontent. The world of the *Aeneid* does not have Homeric remoteness, and Aeneas' grief is not defined by the exempla and tints of heroic poetry. Vergil makes us understand this world and this grief through the violence and innocence of real life.

We can turn, finally, to the death of Euryalus. Vergil defines his death as he does Creusa's, as both the end of innocence and a casualty of realities that Catullus insists pervade the adult world. Euryalus dies

> purpureus veluti cum flos succisus aratro
> languescit moriens, lassove papavera collo
> demisere caput pluvia cum forte gravantur.

[. . . as a purple flower, cut down by the plow, fades as it dies or as poppies droop their heads on weary necks when they chance to be beaten down by rain.]

(*A.* 9.435–37)

The sources for Vergil's simile are well known.[76] Most relevant for the

---

72. The second word in line 21 is in the last position in 22, and *matris,* the last word in 21, is in second position in line 22.

73. Cf. lines 8–9, 12–13, 60–61.

74. Catullus describes this dissolution at length; see Clausen 1977.

75. See "The Death of Pallas" in chapter 4.

76. Conington (1963, *ad loc.*) cites Catullus 11.22–24 and 62.40, with *Il.* 8.306–8; see Johnson 1976, 59–66, for a discussion of these and other Homeric similes (as part of a different argument).

present discussion is Catullus 11, in which the poet describes the death of *amor* because of Lesbia's inconstancy:[77]

> nec meum respectet, ut ante, amorem,
> qui illius culpa cecidit velut prati
> ultimi flos, praetereunte postquam
>   tactus aratro est.

[And let her not look back to my love, as she has done before: my love has died because of her wrong, like a flower that droops at the edge of a meadow when it has been grazed by a passing plow.]

(11.21–24)

The stanza expresses the oppositions that characterize so much of Catullus' poetry, which I have discussed in chapter 2. Catullus' *amor* belongs to a world that is set apart and innocent, *prati ultimi*. Opposed to this private world is the greater world, thronged with adulterers, where true love cannot exist and false love thrives:

> cum suis vivat valeatque moechis,
> quos simul complexa tenet trecentos,
> nullum amans vere, sed identidem omnium
>   ilia rumpens.

[Let her live and thrive with her adulterers, all three hundred of whom she embraces at the same time, loving none truly, but breaking the loins of all again and again.]

(11.17–20)

Catullus here appropriates the image of the flower from the stock of epithalamia (Sappho, Calvus, and Catullus' own wedding poems provide parallels)[78] and represents his affair with Lesbia, once her betrayals begin, as if it is a marriage; by the same conceit, therefore, her lovers are adulterers, *moechis*. Because of her infidelities Catullus becomes like a bride, thrust out of his sanctuary of true love—a child, that is, thrust from innocence into the world of falseness and despair. These oppositions are familiar: Catullus laments the fallen world of the present day and his own (professed) life experience, in which all innocence and everything marvelous and singular are inevitably destroyed. *Amor* and its suggestions of remoteness and isolation are replaced, after Lesbia's be-

---

77. For discussion of Catullus 11 see Ross 1969, 173–75.
78. Cf. Sappho frag. 105 Lobel-Page; Calvus frag. 4; for Catullus see "The Death of Pallas" in chapter 4.

trayal, by the vaster world through which the poet and his companions must now wander to deliver their *non bona dicta*. Here, too, the process of decline continues, as the catalog of exotic and poetic lands, *sive in Hyrcanos Arabasque molles, / seu Sagas sagittiferosve Parthos* [whether you will go among the Hyrcani and the Arabs, the soft race, or among the Sagae or the Parthians, famed archers] (11.5–6), undergoes a leveling degeneration to the familiar landscapes of real-life politics: *sive trans altas gradietur Alpes / Caesaris visens monimenta magni* [or whether you will travel across the high Alps, going to look upon the achievements of great Caesar] (11.9–10).

Euryalus' domestic world—his youth, his beauty, and the lingering mutual dependency of mother and son—and Catullus' *amor* are incompatible with the greater worlds of each poem, defined explicitly by Catullus and suggestively by Vergil as the common experience of life in Rome. Euryalus' departure from his mother and participation in the night mission become the death of innocence in a corrupt world (like the death of *amor*), and his initiation from childhood to adulthood is a travesty of natural growth.

The episode contains a final allusion to Catullus: Euryalus' mother laments his death from the Trojan battlements, *heu, terra ignota canibus data praeda Latinis / alitibusque iaces* [alas, you lie dead in a strange land, spoils for the dogs and carrion birds of Latium] (*A.* 9.485–86), as Ariadne in Catullus 64 laments her abandonment, *dilaceranda feris dabor alitibusque / praeda* [I will be given as spoils for the wild beasts and birds to rend] (64.152–53).[79] The suggestion of Ariadne in Euryalus complements Vergil's borrowing from Catullus 11: Ariadne is made an exemplum of the realities that inevitably await one at the passing of childhood and that pervade and define adult life. Euryalus' death is hereby given the same significance: the passing of childhood and the crushing betrayals of the world at large.

---

79. For Catullus' use of *Il.* 1.5 see Renehan 1979; for Vergil's use of Catullus see Thomas 1979. Cf. Zetzel 1978.

CHAPTER IV

Pallas

Vergil's account of Aeneas and Pallas (Books 8–10) frames the episode of Nisus and Euryalus in Book 9 and reproduces in larger scale and with broader significance the themes of the miniature at its center. Aeneas' tutelage of Pallas and the introduction of the younger hero to the world of the older is presented as an assault on innocence, and Pallas' death is a violation of a figurative childhood. The *puer*, innocent and inexperienced, is drawn to the attractions of heroism; the rewards and values of the heroic world emerge as illusions, which threaten and finally destroy childhood and the values it represents.[1]

Pallas' childhood differs significantly from the childhood of Euryalus. Euryalus' *amor* with Nisus, his innocence and isolation, and the domestic ideal represented by his connection to his mother are antithetical to warfare, and the tragedy of Euryalus turns on his unsuitability for the heroic world: he is out of context in battle and the throng of heroes, and in his death we feel the passing of simplicity and delicacy, the destruction of an ideal of *amor*. Pallas, both by character and background, and by his many and clear affinities with Sarpedon and Patroklos in the *Iliad*,[2] should affirm the heroic ethos; he is the ideal heroic youth.[3] Most important, he belongs to the Roman future (as Euryalus belongs to the Trojan past): he is particularly associated with Marcellus (*miserande puer*, A. 6.882 = 11.42), and like Marcellus, he should have lived to become a cornerstone of the Roman state: *ei mihi quantum / praesidium, Ausonia, et quantum tu per-*

---

1. Thematic exigencies affect Vergil's treatment of the peoples of Italy. Latium, for the purposes of the Trojan "assault," is said to be long accustomed to peace: *rex arva Latinus et urbes / iam senior longa placidas in pace regebat* (A. 7.45–46). The narrative demands, however, that a second Iliad and a new Achilles cannot plausibly emerge in a bucolic retreat; warriors are needed for a battle narrative, and so in the description of the Arcadians an "inconsistency" appears: *hi [Arcades] bellum adsidue ducunt cum gente Latina* (A. 8.55). The same theme of the assault on innocence obliges Vergil to exaggerate the degree of Pallas' youth and inexperience: like Euryalus, he is not literally a *puer*, and he is not wholly innocent of warfare and the world outside Pallanteum.

2. For parallels and discussion see Knauer 1964, 298–301.

3. Heinze 1915, 216: "der ideale Jüngling."

dis, Iule (*A.* 11.57–58).[4] The tragedy of Pallas is that he fails and dies despite his rightness for the heroic world—for some world other than that of the *Aeneid*—in which heroic conventions and values still have meaning.

Vergil makes the themes of childhood and adulthood the foundation for a more general depiction of cultural decline. The arrival of the Trojans in Evander's kingdom (*A.* 8.86–101) alludes to the beginning of Catullus 64: Aeneas' ships are the first to sail on the Tiber, *mirantur et undae, / miratur nemus* (*A.* 8.91–92), just as the Nereides wonder at the first ship in the world (*admirantes,* 64.15).[5] The implications of this reference have been studied in some detail: Vergil suggests the start of a new age in Italy parallel to the new age begun by the voyage of the Argo; and as the Argo ushers in the "iron age" of heroes, so we anticipate that the appearance of heroes and epic deeds in the new world of Latium will also mean (in certain ways) the end of innocence and harmony and the start of treachery and bloodshed.[6] Traditional heroism and its manners emerge here, as they do in Vergil's night episode, as deceptions cloaked in darkness; here, too, the people and places are not larger than life or remote: their losses and suffering are the experience of Vergil's own world, and Catullus is again the touchstone.

THE HEROIC EDUCATION OF PALLAS

We can begin by considering the qualities of Pallas' childhood. Vergil describes Pallas' first meeting with Aeneas by a narrative doublet. The young prince has never been to war (*A.* 10.508), but he knows the stories of the Trojan War and is fired by what he has heard of the Dardanidae: *obstipuit tanto percussus nomine Pallas* [Pallas was astounded, struck by so famous a name] (*A.* 8.121).[7] Vergil says nothing else of his reaction; the rest is suggested by Evander's subsequent account of his own meeting as a young man with Anchises (*A.* 8.154–68), and from the old man's description of the past we are left to imagine the character and reactions of his son in the present. This doublet serves narrative economy but also

---

4. Cf. *A.* 6.872–74, and the similarities of Anchises' eulogy for Marcellus and Aeneas' for Pallas.

5. Noted by Gransden 1976, *ad A.* 8.91–92, and Thomas 1982a, 160–61.

6. Wiesen 1973, Thomas 1982a, 160, and 1982b, 93–107.

7. Compare, for language and sense, Euryalus' response to the call to heroism: *obstipuit magno laudum percussus amore* (*A.* 9.197–98).

implies a pattern of young men invested by the previous generation (and by men other than their fathers) with heroic ideals. The details in Evander's account conform to Vergil's description of Euryalus: like Euryalus (and Pallas), Evander was then a young man poised between childhood and adulthood, *tum mihi prima genas vestibat flore iuventas* [then the first down of youth covered my cheeks with its bloom] (*A.* 8.160; cf. *A.* 9.181), attracted to the emblems of heroic success, and susceptible to the influence of an older hero. Arms and finery attract Euryalus; Evander, too, delighted in Anchises' arrows, cloaks woven with gold, and golden bridles, and he has passed on the bridles to Pallas (*A.* 8.166–68). Like Evander, Euryalus and now Pallas enter the epic world under a hero's guidance.

Pallas, Evander, and Heracles

Pallas reflects the cultural innocence of Evander and of the Arcadians. He is Evander's hope of the race, *spes et solacia nostri* [my hope for the future and my comfort] (*A.* 8.514), and he expects to imitate his father's deeds and heroism: *per spemque meam, patriae quae nunc subit aemula laudi* [by my hope that now rises up, a rival to the praise my father won] (*A.* 10.371). Evander approves (in contrast to Euryalus' mother's disapproval) and even welcomes his son's attraction and introduction to martial deeds and glory,[8] and he invests Pallas with the heroic ideals of the primitive community. He begins his farewell to his son (*A.* 8.560–84) with a lament for his own lost youth, reminiscing that as a young man he had killed Erulus, a fabulous creature with three lives (*A.* 8.560–67). In his reminiscing we recognize Homer's aging statesmen (Nestor, for example, to whom Evander here is usually compared)[9] and also the emergence of a larger theme. Evander's heroic world is a mythical realm of monstrous creatures, heroic labors, and clear moral choices, and it is to evoke this past age of heroism that Vergil includes Evander's story of Erulus (perhaps invents it, since we know the story from no other source)[10] as a lesser version of Heracles' fight with Geryon. The resemblances are obvious, and Geryon is in our mind throughout the episode: Heracles is driving

---

8. See *A.* 11.154–55: *haud ignarus eram quantum nova gloria in armis / et praedulce decus primo certamine posset* [I knew how strong was the pull of newfound glory in arms and of the cherished honor of first battle]; and cf. *A.* 8.510.

9. I.e., *Il.* 7.132–35 and 11.670–81; see Knauer 1964, 451 and 462.

10. See Fordyce 1977, *ad A.* 8.563.

Geryon's cattle at the time of Cacus' theft; Erulus is thrice-lived, *nascenti cui tris animas Feronia mater . . . dederat* [his mother, Feronia, had given him three lives at birth] (*A.* 8.564), and Geryon is triple-bodied (*tergeminus, A.* 8.202).[11] These are the models of good and evil that Evander presses upon Aeneas as he exhorts him to simplicity and heroism:

> [Evander] 'haec' inquit 'limina victor
> Alcides subiit, haec illum regia cepit.
> aude, hospes, contemnere opes et te quoque dignum
> finge deo, rebusque veni non asper egenis.'

[Then Evander spoke: "Heracles the conqueror bent for this doorway, and this royal house received him. Be bold enough, my guest-friend, to disdain wealth and, as he did, make yourself worthy of heaven; do not be too proud for our poor home."]

(A. 8.362–65)

These are the models that Evander's account of Erulus and of the deeds of his youth implicitly holds up before Pallas. Pallas' innocence, therefore, reflects Evander's, and as the episode progresses the distance grows between Evander's vision of heroism and the reality that awaits Pallas outside the cultural sanctuary of Pallanteum.

Aeneas' journey to Evander's kingdom, the *res inopes* (A. 8.100), is a movement into the cultural past—a movement, that is, away from Troy and the civilized world of navigation, away from the world of shields and painted hulls that are so out of place in the groves and rivers of Pallanteum. This journey is also defined metaphorically as a return to youth, and Vergil gradually develops the association between childhood and cultural innocence by a series of allusions to the *Odyssey*. Vergil (as has long been recognized) compares Aeneas' arrival in Pallanteum with Telemachus' journey in search of Odysseus.[12] The Arcadians sacrifice to Heracles on the shore as Aeneas disembarks, just as Nestor in Pylos is sacrificing to Poseidon as Telemachus arrives; and Pallas comes forward to greet the Trojan strangers, as Nestor's son, Peisistratos, welcomes Telemachus (*Od.* 3.36–42). We can attribute some of these resemblances to the

---

11. Servius (*ad A.* 8.564) makes the connection: *attendum sane, hoc sibi Evandrum vindicare quod fuit in Hercule; nam ut ille Geryonem extinxit, ita hic Erylum occidit* [It is clear, of course, that Evander claims for himself what had happened in the case of Heracles; for as Heracles killed Geryon, he himself slew Erulus].

12. See Knauer 1964, 249–55 for discussion, 403–5 for references, and Klingner 1967, 530–34.

"formulaic" composition of arrival scenes,[13] but the portrait of Aeneas also contains suggestions of Telemachus' arrival in Sparta (*Od.* 4.20–403) and of his return to Ithaka (*Od.* 16).[14] Vergil seems to insist that we associate the two characters: Aeneas, the adult hero of the poem, becomes like a boy on the verge of manhood as he returns to this oasis of cultural innocence.

Other allusions to Homer confirm the suggestion that cultural innocence is a metaphorical youth. Evander rises on the morning of Aeneas' departure and leaves his simple quarters, *ex humili tecto* (*A.* 8.455), dressed in animal hides as a primitive, *demissa ab laeva pantherae terga retorquens* [twisting back from his left shoulder the hide of a panther] (*A.* 8.460), while birds sing in the rooftops, *et matutini volucrum sub culmine cantus* [the morning songs of birds rose from under the eaves] (*A.* 8.456).[15] The description also owes many details to Homeric passages, and we find, as we might expect, Evander compared with the elder characters of the Homeric poems, Menelaus (in the *Odyssey*) and Nestor.[16] Vergil adds another detail, however, which is more difficult to account for:

> nec non et gemini custodes limine ab alto
> praecedunt gressumque canes comitantur erilem.

[The two dogs preceded him from the threshold and accompanied their master as he went.]

(*A.* 8.461–62)

Commentaries compare Evander to Telemachus, also accompanied by his dogs on the morning he leaves Ithaka to search for his father (*Od.* 2.11–12).[17] The same formula occurs twice more in Homer (*Od.* 17.62 and 20.145), both times describing Telemachus.[18] With the *Telemachia* so repeatedly invoked it is unlikely that these lines are merely epic "ornamentation" and that Vergil is not working purposefully. Evander is compared to a boy on his first venture into manhood because Vergil equates the innocence of Telemachus' youth with the cultural innocence of Evander and with his vision of the heroic world.

---

13. See Clausen 1987, 67–69; for general similarities compare Ap. Rh. *Argo.* 2.752–814, and "The Child and the Hero" in chapter 1.
14. See Knauer 1964, 252, for discussion.
15. For birds and precivilized isolation see "The Death of Euryalus" and n. 66 in chapter 4.
16. Knauer (1964, 404–5) compares Evander with Menelaus (*Od.* 4.308) and with Nestor (*Il.* 2.42–47).
17. E.g., Conington 1963, *ad loc.*
18. See Knauer 1964, 405.

Dido and Laomedon

Pallas' youth and inexperience reflect the character of Pallanteum, and he stands ready to inherit the heroic ideals of the past, the past to which Evander belongs and that he repeatedly evokes. Evander recalls his first meeting with Priam and Anchises as his introduction to the heroic world:

> nam memini Hesionae visentem regna sororis
> Laomedontiaden Priamum Salamina petentem
> protinus Arcadiae gelidos invisere finis.
> tum mihi prima genas vestibat flore iuventas,
> mirabarque duces Teucros, mirabar et ipsum
> Laomedontiaden; sed cunctis altior ibat
> Anchises.

[I remember that Priam, Laomedon's son, while traveling to Salamis, the kingdom of his sister Hesione, came to visit the cold borders of Arcadia. At the time the first down of youth was just covering my cheeks with its bloom; I marveled at the Trojan generals, and at Priam, Laomedon's son; but Anchises stood taller than all the rest.]

                                                                    (*A*. 8.157–63)

This passage is a perfect heroic vignette, full of Homeric figures and diction,[19] including Priam's patronymic in its Greek form, *Laomedontiaden*, twice in five lines.

Evander's reminiscences of legendary events and distant places, however, include details that suggest that his ideals are fantasies, youthful illusions relived in and sustained by old age; these illusions studiously avoid but inexorably draw our attention to the "reality" of Troy and its persistent associations. Commentaries, first of all, connect Evander's speech to Dido's first meeting with Aeneas and her recall of her earlier meeting with Teucer (*A*. 1.619–24);[20] Evander's repeated *Laomedontiaden* brings to mind the exemplar of Trojan deceit, who figured as well in Dido's condemnation of Aeneas.[21] More striking, Evander's recollections are fragments of a larger narrative in which Laomedon attempted to cheat Heracles: Laomedon chained his daughter Hesione outside the walls of Troy as an offering to a sea serpent who was ravaging the countryside; when Heracles offered to free her for a price, Laomedon agreed,

---

19. See Knauer 1964, 403, and Fordyce 1977, *ad loc.*
20. See Conington 1963 and Austin 1971, both *ad A*. 1.619.
21. Cf. *A*. 4.541; for Vergil's Laomedon see further *A*. 3.248 and *G*. 1.501–2, and see Wiesen 1973, 744–46.

but reneged.[22] Vergil thus glosses the start of the Arcadian and Trojan alliance by these reminders of present and past Trojan duplicity, Aeneas' of Dido and Laomedon's of Heracles. These undertones and intimations are all the more inescapable given that the latter deception is of the very patron whose deeds the Arcadians celebrate as Aeneas arrives and whose exploits include an earlier sacking of Troy:

> hic iuvenum chorus, ille senum, qui carmine laudes
> Herculeas et facta ferunt: ut prima novercae
> monstra manu geminosque premens eliserit anguis,
> ut bello egregias idem disiecerit urbes,
> Troiamque Oechaliamque.

[On one side the chorus of young men, on the other side the chorus of elders, who tell in song the glorious deeds of Heracles and his labors: how first he throttled with his hands the twin snakes, monsters sent by his stepmother, and how next he made war, bringing to ruin famed cities, Troy and Oechalia.]

(A. 8.287–91)

Some effort has been made to explain away Vergil's emphatic reference to Laomedon. It has been argued that Priam and Anchises represent the bad and the good, respectively, of the legacy of Troy:[23]

> Dem neuen Troia wird die Schuld des alten nicht mehr anhaften. Die Nachkommen des Anchises werden—vereinigt mit den Latinern—das neue Troia grunden und einst die Welt beherrschen.

Against this interpretation is Aeneas' epithet *Laomedontius* at the beginning of Book 8 (line 18). Nowhere else in the poem is the epithet used of him, and it implies that he, not just Priam or Priam's line, carries the *periuria* and *scelera* of the Trojan past. Vergil suggests in this passage, therefore, as he does throughout the episode, that Pallas' vision of heroism in the figure of Aeneas consists of the same illusions as those of the young Evander (to which he still seems to cling in his old age), and that instead of finding traditional heroic nobility, Pallas will enter a world that "Laomedon" characterizes.

Other critics argue that *Laomedontius* can mean simply "Trojan"[24] and,

22. Heracles kills Laomedon and sends Hesione to Salamis to marry Telemon (see Servius *ad A.* 8.157).

23. Binder 1971, 70–71.

24. I am inclined to agree with Wiesen's (1973, 745) view that the name is too consistently negative in Vergil's poetry to be a colorless synonym for "Trojan."

in particular, that *Laomedontius* at *Aeneid* 8.18 is a neutral use of the name with none of its usual connotations.[25] Vergil follows the epithet, however, with highly compressed suggestions of a world in which Laomedon and bad faith are typical features:

> talia per Latium. quae Laomedontius heros
> cuncta videns magno curarum fluctuat aestu,
> atque animum nunc huc celerem nunc dividit illuc
> in partisque rapit varias perque omnia versat.

[Such were the events in Latium. Aeneas, descended from Laomedon, was tossed on great tides of care as he watched it all, and he turned his mind hurriedly now to one matter, now to another; he weighed every possibility and chance, pondered every detail.]

(*A.* 8.18–21)

Though "tides of care" is a conventional figure,[26] Vergil's language may suggest Catullus and call to mind Ariadne's grief at Theseus' desertion, *magnis curarum fluctuat undis* (64.62). We are, furthermore, twice reminded of Dido: first, of her sleeplessness on the night Aeneas slips away and of her resolve to kill herself, *magno . . . fluctuat aestu* (*A.* 4.532); second, of Aeneas' fear and indecision after Hermes' admonition in Book 4 (*A.* 8.20–21 = *A.* 4.285–86). With these suggestions in the air Vergil begins his account of Aeneas' alliance with Evander and of the heroic education of Pallas. The funeral of Pallas refers again to the desertion of Dido (see "The Death of Pallas" in this chapter); like the initiation of Euryalus, the episode begins and ends with allusions to the poem's great exemplum of deception and loss.

Loss and the Domestic World

Though Pallas' childhood reflects the innocence of Pallanteum and the heroic values of the past, Pallas never becomes a "symbol" or an abstraction. Evander sends his son into dangers that are peculiarly Vergilian and that link the father and son relationship with other kinds of relationships in the poem: parents and children (Euryalus and his mother) and lovers (Dido and Aeneas). Evander fears for his son's safety and prays to die if Pallas is fated not to return from battle:

> nunc, nunc o liceat crudelem abrumpere vitam,

---

25. Fordyce 1977, *ad A.* 7.105, following Conington 1963, *ad loc.*
26. See Gransden 1976, *ad A.* 8.19–21, and Kroll 1968, *ad* 64.62.

dum curae ambiguae, dum spes incerta futuri,
dum te, care puer, mea sola et sera voluptas,
complexu teneo, gravior neu nuntius auris
vulneret.

[Would that I could right now cut short cruel life, now, while my fears
are still uncertain, while hope is still possible, while I still hold you in
my arms, dear son, my only joy, given to me so late in life; would that I
could die before my ears suffer some report that harm has come to you.]
(A. 8.579–83)

Vergil connects Evander's farewell to Pallas with the lament of Euryalus'
mother at her son's death (A. 9.482–97). Evander's prayer for death is repeated by Euryalus' mother (A. 8.579 = A. 9.497), and we may compare
the sense, if not the words, of Evander's description of his son, *mea sola
et sera voluptas*, with her description of Euryalus, *senectae sera meae requies*
(A. 9.482).[27] Both characters consider the lives of their children life itself,
and both mourn the end of the *requies* and *voluptas* of the domestic world
and familial love.[28] I discussed in the previous chapter the connection
between this lament by Euryalus' mother and Dido's words to Aeneas on
the morning of his departure from Carthage.[29] Both women have lost
their love to the larger world of the poem, and each feels her loss to be a
betrayal. Playing on this theme of domestic loss Vergil also connects
Evander's farewell to Pallas with Dido's despair at Aeneas' departure.
Evander's prayers for his son's life and safety end abruptly:

haec genitor digressu dicta supremo
fundebat; famuli conlapsum in tecta ferebant.

[In a last farewell father Evander spoke this flood of words and fell to
the ground; his servants carried him within.]
(A. 8.583–84)

The scene repeats Dido's collapse at the end of her speech to Aeneas as
he leaves Carthage for Italy:

---

27. Words approximated, furthermore, in Amata's plea to Turnus: *spes tu nunc una,
senectae / tu requies miserae* (A. 12.57–58); see "Dido and Amata" in chapter 4.

28. Catullus lingers on the same theme: cf. Aegeus' farewell to Theseus and the explicit
contrast between familial love—*gnate mihi longa iucundior unice vita* [son, dearer to me
than even long life] (64.215)—and the devastating effects of the heroic world—*quandoqui-
dem fortuna mea ac tua fervida virtus / eripit invito mihi te* [since my ill fortune and your
burning manhood tears you away from me, against my will] (218–19); see "The *lusus
Troiae*" in chapter 5.

29. Cf. A. 4.584–85 with A. 9.459–60, and "Dido" in chapter 3.

suscipiunt famulae conlapsaque membra
marmoreo referunt thalamo stratisque reponunt.

[Serving women took her up, bearing her powerless limbs to the marble
bedroom, and placed her on the bed.]

(A. 4.391–92)

The features of this theme are clear: Pallas, like Euryalus and Aeneas,
abandons the domestic world of love and security for the demands of
heroism; and like Euryalus' mother and Dido, Evander, too, falls victim
to the world of the poem.

Aeneas' betrayal of Dido is the paradigm for the conflict between love
and the character of the world of the *Aeneid,* and Vergil invokes this paradigm again and again. The possibility of correctly choosing between
Dido and fate is not Vergil's concern, nor is Aeneas' guilt or innocence,
as most critics now concede; Vergil instead describes the irresolvable
clash between love and the epic world's demands.

This paradigm emerges throughout the poem in a variety of forms,
and one further example is especially noteworthy. The portrait of Brutus
and his sons in the underworld repeats the themes of Dido and Aeneas,
depicting the same clash between love and the *causa publica,* and the same
result.

natosque pater nova bella moventis
ad poenam pulchra pro libertate vocabit,
infelix, utcumque ferent ea facta minores:
vincet amor patriae laudumque immensa cupido.

[Brutus, a father, when his own sons urge wars of rebellion, will demand
their punishment to protect noble liberty—an unhappy and solitary
man, no matter how later generations will relate these deeds: love of
country will overwhelm him, and an unconquerable desire for praise.]

(A. 6.820–23)

Natosque pater is a significant juxtaposition, with variations appearing
frequently in scenes of familial closeness or tragic separation;[30] and *infelix*
perhaps suggests not only unhappiness but also the lack of progeny (here
through loss).[31] In the *Aeneid* the love between parents and children (and

---

30. Cf. *nato genetrix, A.* 1.590, with Austin's (1971) note; *genitor natum, A.* 10.466; *genitor
nati, A.* 10.800; and cf. *genitoris filia,* Catullus 64.117, with Kroll 1968, *ad loc.* For discussion
see Clausen 1977, 219–20.

31. As often elsewhere in Vergil: see Pease 1935, *ad A.* 4.68; for *felix* see Norden 1957,
ad A. 6.783.

the domestic world generally) cannot coexist with the *virtus* of civic life.[32]

This passage is among the most important in the poem: the phrase *vincet amor patriae* is a variation on a theme that Vergil uses in climactic passages in each of his previous works. At the end of the *Eclogues* love is a fatal affliction that causes the dissolution of the pastoral world, and neither poetry nor science can provide remedies against it: *omnia vincit Amor* (*Ecl.* 10.69);[33] the affliction and the phrase are transformed, in turn, to the themes of the *Georgics, labor omnia vicit* (*G.* 1.145–46).[34] In *Aeneid* 6 Vergil brings this motif out of the landscapes of the *Eclogues* and the *Georgics* and shapes it to the social and political themes of his epic: men are still undone by recurring and invincible destruction, now in its epic incarnation: *vincet amor patriae*.[35]

It is important that we not rationalize the suffering of Dido, Evander, and Brutus (the commonplace, for example, that the founding of a new state will inevitably have costs) or invent consolations where Vergil insists that there are none: *infelix, utcumque ferent ea facta minores* (*A.* 6.822). As in the case of Aeneas and Dido, Vergil neither censures Brutus nor condemns the demands of statehood; he offers no solution to the dilemma, no acceptable choice. The world Vergil describes in his poem produces irreconcilable demands between correct, or "heroic," action (*laudumque immensa cupido*) and love. In this new world, the realities of the *causa publica*—the founding, establishment, and preservation of the Roman state—clash fundamentally with the love between fathers and sons (Brutus and his sons, Evander and Pallas), erotic love (Dido and Aeneas), and even, as I show in the next section of this chapter, social alliances (the *hospitium* between Aeneas and Pallas).

THE INITIATION OF PALLAS

Idealized heroic values ostensibly await Pallas at his initiation, and his death represents the failure of these values in the world of the epic. Because he has never fought before (*A.* 10.508), he is entrusted by Evander to Aeneas for his education in warfare and in adulthood:

---

32. Polybius (6.54) suggests that fathers condemning their sons is a characteristically Roman sort of civic piety; e.g., Val. Max. 5.8.3–5 and Accius *Brutus.*

33. See Ross 1975, 85–106.

34. See further Ross 1987, 104 and 171, and Thomas 1988b, vol. 1, *ad loc.*

35. Compare Aeneas' words to Dido, *hic amor, haec patria est* (*A.* 4.347), quoted under "Dido and Amata" in this chapter.

hunc tibi praeterea, spes et solacia nostri,
Pallanta adiungam; sub te tolerare magistro
militiam et grave Martis opus, tua cernere facta
adsuescat, primis et te miretur ab annis.

[I shall add Pallas to your ranks as well, my hope for the future and my
comfort; let him grow accustomed, with you as his teacher, to endure
the warrior's life and the painful duty of battle and to watch your deeds;
let him wonder at you from his earliest years.]

(A. 8.514–17)

Evander's words in some sense define life as Aeneas experiences it: a succession of *labores* (*militiam, grave opus, facta*) that one must learn to endure (*tolerare, cernere . . . adsuescat*). We are an appreciable distance here from Evander's reminiscing about the marvels of his youth and his longing to do battle again with monsters: Pallas leaves his father alone and bereft, and he goes out to fight, not on mythic battlefields as a smaller, younger Heracles against another Cacus or Erulus, but against Mezentius, whom Vergil takes pains to make a terrible but human enemy,[36] and against Turnus. Aeneas' reaction to Evander's words spreads gloom over the proceedings:

defixique ora tenebant
Aeneas Anchisiades et fidus Achates,
multaque dura suo tristi cum corde putabant.

[Aeneas, son of Anchises, and faithful Achates stood stunned and kept
silent, pondering with grieving hearts the many hardships ahead.]

(A. 8.520–22)

Critics have suggested that the use of Aeneas' patronymic *Anchisiades* (521) foreshadows Pallas' death.[37]

It is remarkable that Vergil does not show us Pallas fighting at Aeneas' side (as Euryalus fights beside Nisus) or any literal enactment of Evander's charge to Aeneas. He places in the foreground, instead, the thematic associations of the transition from childhood to adulthood, and the values that each implies. Pallas' transformation from Evander's son in Pallanteum in Book 8 to a warrior with a brief *aristeia* and death in Book 10 is mediated by only a few lines:

---

36. Even at his monstrous worst (binding living men to corpses) Mezentius is
apparently modeled on a historical figure; see Fordyce 1977, *ad A.* 8.487.
37. So Putnam 1965, 142–43; Wiesen 1973, 758; and Gransden 1976, *ad A.* 8.521–22.

> hic magnus sedet Aeneas secumque volutat
> eventus belli varios, Pallasque sinistro
> adfixus lateri iam quaerit sidera, opacae
> noctis iter, iam quae passus terraque marique.

[There great Aeneas sat and pondered all the possible turns of the war;
Pallas, clinging close by his left side, asked now about the stars, their
guides through the dark night, now what Aeneas had endured on land
and sea.]

(*A.* 10.159–62)

Aeneas faces uncertainties with characteristic preoccupation and doubt
(cf. *A.* 6.185 and *A.* 8.520–22) in contrast to Pallas' youthful enthusiasm:
adfixus is strong for "sat next to" (see Conington, *ad loc.*), and the asyn-
detic *iam quaerit sidera . . . iam quae passus* suggests his eagerness and wonder.

It is no surprise that Pallas asks about heroic deeds; the same process
is described in the fourth *Eclogue* as the *puer* learns about the iron age
world that awaits him.[38] But why does Pallas ask about the stars? It adds,
certainly, to the portrait of youthful inexperience, but there is further
point in the appositive phrase *opacae / noctis iter. Sidera* are not objects of
natural wonder in the present passage; they are a navigational tool, *iter,*
a use implicitly foreign to Pallanteum and the Arcadian people (cf. *A.*
8.91–93). As such they belong to the world of epic deeds that Pallas is
about to enter: the *puer* knows nothing about them; only Aeneas, the
adult hero, understands their use.[39] Navigation traditionally characterizes the iron age,[40] with special prominence in the versions of Catullus
(64.1–21) and Vergil. In the first *Georgic* the age of Saturn ends and Jupiter's reign begins, accompanied by the *artes* of civilization:

> tunc alnos primum fluvii sensere cavatas;
> navita tum stellis numeros et nomina fecit
> Pleiadas, Hyadas, claramque Lycaonis Arcton.

[Then for the first time rivers felt the alders hollowed into boats; then
the sailor discerned the constellations among the stars and gave them
names, Pleiades, Hyades, and the shining bear of Lycaon.]

(*G.* 1.136–38)

---

38. *At simul heroum laudes et facta parentis / iam legere et quae sit poteris cognoscere
virtus . . .* [But, child, as soon as you are able to read the exploits of heroes and the deeds
of your father and to learn what manhood means . . .] (*Ecl.* 4.26–27).

39. Compare Nisus' survival in the dark woods and Euryalus' failure; see "Troy and
Childhood" in chapter 3.

40. See Nisbet and Hubbard 1970, on Horace, *Odes* 1.3.12.

We can compare again the fourth *Eclogue*, and the vestigial effects of Trojan *prisca fraus* on the boy as he approaches adulthood:

> pauca tamen suberunt priscae vestigia fraudis,
> quae temptare Thetim ratibus, quae cingere muris
> oppida, quae iubeant telluri infindere sulcos.
> alter erit tum Tiphys et altera quae vehat Argo
> delectos heroas.

[Even so, a few traces of our ancestral treachery will lie hidden, which will bid us venture on the sea in ships, ring our cities with walls, dig furrows in the earth. There will be another Tiphys, and another Argo will carry picked heroes.]

(*Ecl.* 4.31–35)

These parallels imply, first, that the stars (as *noctis iter*) and the struggles of the adult (*quae passus terraque marique*) constitute the "iron age" realities to which Aeneas introduces Pallas[41] (the iron ages of Hesiod, Aratus, and Vergil, after all, are merely conceits for each author's own place and time); and second, that the fabulous deeds and mythical creatures that Evander recollects and that Pallas anticipates do not exist.

Vergil makes this suggestion by still another detail. Night is associated elsewhere in Vergil's poetry with treachery and death. It figures in the fourth *Georgic* and Orpheus' journey to the underworld, and it has further implications in the *Aeneid*, both in Vergil's night episode and in the fall of Troy in the second book, where it is associated with *fraus* and *insidiae*.[42] It is appropriate, therefore, that Pallas' passage to adulthood occurs at night, and there is no need here for Vergil to develop this theme at length: the *facta heroum* and the *Martis opus* are what Pallas must come to know and learn to endure, and darkness, *opaca nox*, is their element.

The collocation *nox opaca* occurs only twice elsewhere in the *Aeneid*, both times in scenes of deception: the "night" (i.e., the storm) of Dido and Aeneas' "marriage" (*A.* 4.123) and the night of the Gallic attack on the Capitoline (*A.* 8.658). The treachery that haunts the poem, therefore, may be suggested by the same phrase in this passage and may further define

41. Hardie (1986) collects versions of this tripartite summary of the universe—*sidera, terra, mare*—and argues convincingly that they comprise a "motif of the hero at the mercy of the elements" (331; see further 293–335).

42. See "The Initiation of Euryalus" in chapter 3.

the world that Pallas enters as filled with deceptions and finally destructive.[43]

Heracles, Aeneas, and Augustus

Vergil builds analogies between childhood, cultural innocence, and an anachronistic ideal of heroism through the characters of Pallas, Evander, and Heracles; he further suggests that cultural innocence and its heroic ideals are illusions that, like childhood, cannot exist in the world of the *Aeneid*. This distinction between heroism and the world of the epic obliges us to reconsider the Heracles and Cacus epyllion in Book 8 and its meaning for Vergil's contemporaries.

Heracles' adoption and rehabilitation by various philosophical sects in the late Republic is well known, and the suggestion that Heracles is Vergil's model for Aeneas and, furthermore, a heroic exemplar for Augustus, is now a familiar part of criticism.[44] One of the standard commentaries on *Aeneid* 8, for example, argues that Vergil

> underline[s] . . . the links between the Roman past and the Roman present, to demonstrate that there is one and the same Rome, and to portray Aeneas, Heracles, Evander and even Saturn as forerunners or 'types' of Augustus. Hercules' conquest over Cacus, Aeneas' victory over Turnus are patterned precursors of Augustus' crushing of Antony.[45]

While a minority consider the passage "a piece of literary technique," an *aetion* without political or moral undertones,[46] many critics detect a different sort of oblique political commentary. The "problems" with the passage—the *furor* exhibited in Heracles' attack and the suggestions of animal savagery in the phrase *dentibus infrendens,* used of both the Cyclops and Mezentius[47]—incline them to see Vergil's depiction as covertly anti-

---

43. According to Norden (1957, *ad A.* 6.195, 208), *opacus,* like *opacare,* often has a sacral and even funereal tone in Vergil's poetry.

44. See Henry 1873–92, vol. 1, *ad A.* 1.14, "tot—labores," pp. 187–95; followed by, e.g., Fränkel 1951; Otis 1963, 334–36; Buchheit 1963, 116–33; and Galinsky 1972, 126–66.

45. Walsh's comments in his introduction to the Fordyce commentary (Fordyce 1977, xxiv–xxv) are balanced and can fairly be called typical (though I will dispute them in what follows).

46. So Fordyce 1977, *ad A.* 8.184–279 (pp. 226–27): "political allusions need not be looked for any more than in the Aristaeus episode of Geo.iv."

47. *A.* 8.230 = *A.* 3.664 (of the Cyclops) = *A.* 10.718 (of a wild boar, in a simile that describes Mezentius).

Augustan: the poet ingeniously subverts current propaganda by which the *princeps* links himself to the greatest mythic hero.[48]

Arguments for nonmeaning (that the passage is "a piece of literary technique") are impossible to answer; one either believes them or not (I do not). But both the pro- and the anti-Augustan views—on the one hand, that Heracles is Vergil's ideal, a model for Augustus (via Aeneas), while Cacus is a veiled Turnus or Antony; on the other hand, that "flaws" in Evander's Heracles represent criticisms of Augustus (*are* they flaws? is there a philosophically correct way to kill a fire-breathing monster?)—ignore the fact that it is Evander who recounts and interprets the legend. Evander holds up these exempla of good and evil to his son and to Aeneas, and Evander's character and his role in the poem must necessarily color our estimate of these models.

The *Aeneid* contains two versions of Heracles and they are distinct and incompatible. Evander's tale is simple and fantastic: storybook heroes and villains clash in glorified cattle raids; evil comes on stage in pure form, breathing fire, and bearing a "significant" name by childish etymologies, Cacus/κακός/*caecus*. Where tradition gives a local shepherd (Livy 1.7.5) or a thief (D.H. 1.39.2), Vergil invents a supernatural *monstrum*, a fitting adversary to Evander's heroic ideal. Heracles is the avenger, *maximus ultor* (line 201), the deliverer (line 189), the same creature of aggression and direct action found throughout the literary tradition.

The other portrait of Heracles, in *Aeneid* 10, bears little resemblance to Evander's; Pallas prays before his duel with Turnus and invokes the aid of his patron:

> per patris hospitium et mensas, quas advena adisti
> te precor, Alcide, coeptis ingentibus adsis.
> cernat semineci sibi me rapere arma cruenta
> victoremque ferant morientia lumina Turni.

[Heracles, by the guest-friendship you enjoy with my father and the tables that you came to as a stranger, I beg you, look with favor on this bold undertaking: let Turnus, wounded and failing, watch me strip off his bloodstained arms, and let him endure, as he dies, the sight of his conqueror.]

(*A.* 10.460–63)

Pallas names services rendered, *hospitium* and *mensas*, in exchange for help and intercession, and he asks for glory or a hero's death. Evander's

---

48. E.g., Wigodsky 1965, 219.

portrayal of Heracles as a giant-killer, along with the formulaic prayer by Evander's son (the terms of his prayer are conventional and unemotional), leave us unprepared for the hero's reaction:

> audiit Alcides iuvenem magnumque sub imo
> corde premit gemitum lacrimasque effundit inanis.

[Alcides heard the youth, checked back deep in his heart a great moan, and poured forth tears shed in vain.]

(A. 10.464–65)

This passage is important, and I will return to it later in this chapter; for now we need only note how Vergil has emphasized the intensity of Heracles' grief, and has created a scene in which his hero is paralyzed, incapable of any effective action.

Heracles in this passage is modeled on Zeus in the *Iliad* (16.459–61) as he weeps blood for his son Sarpedon (the model for Pallas in his *aristeia* and death).[49] *Sub imo / corde premit gemitum* and *lacrimasque effundit inanis* are strong words, and Vergil uses similar language in the fourth book as Aeneas faces Dido's accusations and tries to justify his leaving: *ille Iovis monitis immota tenebat / lumina et obnixus curam sub corde premebat* (A. 4.332), and *mens immota manet, lacrimae volvuntur inanes* (A. 4.448).[50] Zeus' tears for Sarpedon are what we might expect of a father who cannot help his son, and there is nothing surprising about Aeneas in agonies of guilt before Dido; but does this language of helplessness and the suggestion of father and son suit Heracles and Pallas? Surely they do not suit the storybook hero of Evander's tale, a hero never without resource:[51] the slayer of Cacus in Book 8 is out of all proportion to real life, a fiction for old men and children; the character that Vergil shows us in the tenth book is feeling and vulnerable, subject to the same helplessness that afflicts the world at large. The world that Pallas will enter and in which Aeneas must strive and act (and that Augustus will inherit) is more complex than anything Evander's stories suggest, and more painfully and markedly human.

Vergil's direct comparison of Aeneas to Heracles confirms this interpretation of the epyllion. Aeneas feels that he has violated a trust at Pallas' death:

---

49. See Knauer 1964, 416, for full references.
50. Conington 1963, *ad loc.*
51. Evander's praise of Heracles, . . . *non te rationis egentem* (A. 8.299).

> Pallas, Evander, in ipsis
> omnia sunt oculis, mensae quas advena primas
> tunc adiit, dextraeque datae.

[Pallas, Evander, all these memories are before his eyes—the tables that first he came to as a stranger, and the pledges given.]

(*A.* 10.515–17)

The repetition from Pallas' prayer, *mensas, quas advena adisti* (*A.* 10.460–61), equates Aeneas not with Evander's hero but with the "real," grieving Heracles, who is subject to the human realities of sadness and death. This equation is a powerful refutation of conventional heroism: by a remarkable inversion Vergil uses Heracles, the archetypal hero from mythology, to suggest the vulnerability and mere humanity of Aeneas the man.[52] If there is any message for Augustus in the characterizations of Heracles and Aeneas, it is that labor and suffering are inescapable realities for gods, heroes, and men.[53]

We should consider a final contrast between the illusory heroism that Heracles represents and the world of Vergil's poem. Evander praises the simple virtue of (his) Heracles and urges Aeneas to imitate it (*A.* 8.366–69). The passage concludes, however, with different suggestions: *nox ruit et fuscis tellurem amplectitur alis* [night falls, embracing the earth with dark wings] (*A.* 8.369). This conclusion recalls Allecto one book earlier, *protinus hinc fuscis tristis dea tollitur alis* (*A.* 7.408), as she inflames Turnus, Amata, and the Italian countryside. Allecto transforms Latium into a grim and familiar landscape, far different from the fantastic world envisioned by Evander: Aeneas emerges at the end of Book 8 not as Heracles but as Achilles (lines 608–25) fighting over another Helen in a second Troy.

The Death of Pallas

Vergil's use of Catullan imagery in the details of Euryalus' death implies a general pathology for the world of the *Aeneid*. What particularly interests Vergil about Catullus 11 is the contrast between an ideal of *verus amor* (of which the *prati ultimi flos* is an emblem) and the deceptions and betrayals endemic to the real world—the world, that is, as Catullus per-

---

52. Vergil similarly inspires sympathy for Mezentius by comparing him to the Cyclops: at the death of Lausus, Mezentius laments to Rhaebus, his horse, called *hoc decus illi, / hoc solamen erat* (*A.* 10.858–59), just as Polyphemus seeks the consolation of his flocks, *ea sola voluptas / solamenque mali* (*A.* 3.660–61).

53. Heracles' powerlessness to save Pallas gives a certain irony, too, to his role in the Arcadian cult, *maximus ultor* (*A.* 8.201).

ceives it and consistently portrays it. The vulnerability of the flower and the inevitability of its demise gloss the contrast between Euryalus' childhood innocence and the adult reality of Vergil's poem.

Vergil returns to Catullus' imagery to describe Pallas in death. This flower simile, like the one borrowed from Catullus 11 to describe Euryalus' death, is from an equally surprising source, this time an epithalamion. Pallas on his bier is described

> qualem virgineo demessum pollice florem
> seu mollis violae seu languentis hyacinthi,
> cui neque fulgor adhuc nec dum sua forma recessit,
> non iam mater alit tellus virisque ministrat.

[. . . as a blossom cropped by a girl's finger, either of soft violet or drooping hyacinth, whose radiant color and beauty have not yet faded, but the earth, its mother, no longer nourishes it or gives it strength.]

(*A.* 11.68–71)

Most discussions refer to Catullus 62 as Vergil's source;[54] there the bride is described

> ut flos in saeptis secretus nascitur hortis,
> ignotus pecori, nullo convolsus aratro,
> quem mulcent aurae, firmat sol, educat imber;
> multi illum pueri, multae optavere puellae:
> idem cum tenui carptus defloruit ungui,
> nulli illum pueri, nullae optavere puellae.
> sic virgo, dum intacta manet, dum cara suis est;
> cum castum amisit polluto corpore florem,
> nec pueris iucunda manet, nec cara puellis.

[. . . as a flower hidden in a fenced garden, unknown to the flock, uprooted by no plow: the breezes caress it, the sun makes it strong, and the rains bring it into bloom. Many boys want it, and many girls: but the same flower, when plucked by a slender finger, fades and sheds its petals, no boys want it, and no girls. So a young maiden, so long as she remains untouched, is beloved by her family; when she has lost her chaste flower, her body defiled, she remains dear neither to boys nor to girls.]

(62.39–47)

Catullus' image of the girl as a flower is traditional and the sentiment of lines 44–47 commonplace; Catullus, moreover, archaizes rhetorically (the repetitions in lines 42–44) and syntactically (*dum . . . dum,* line 45) to

---

54. Conington 1963, *ad loc.*

enforce these clichés.[55] The inconcinnity in tone and effect between Vergil's somber passage and Catullus' lighter original is typically noted by critics, and Vergil is credited with giving wholly new sense to Catullan imagery, with stripping away, in other words, its meaning in its original context.[56]

This inconcinnity disappears if we understand Catullus' flower in the garden as Vergil understood it, as capturing, that is, the essential oppositions in Catullus' poetry. In poem 62 Catullus portrays markedly separate worlds: as in poem 11, the flower thrives in isolation, *in saeptis secretus . . . hortis;* marriage and the inevitable consequences of adult love belong to the world outside (Catullus' "real" world of disappointments, neglect, and abandonment), and invade the sanctuary of the garden (youth, fidelity, innocence), destroying the flower within. *Nullo convolsus aratro* (line 40) is another figure for this violence, recalling *praetereunte . . . tactus aratro* (11.23–24), and it marks the same decline, from isolation and innocence into the greater world of treachery.

It is this distinction between "worlds" that Vergil alludes to with his version of the *secretus flos.* The image from Catullus' epithalamion pointedly defines Pallas' entry into battle in terms of a larger pathology, as Vergil aligns the oppositions in his episode with those in Catullus' poem. Pallas' youthful inexperience is made a figurative childhood by Vergil, and by this simile he is invested with the peculiarly Catullan conceptualization of childhood: an ideal state of trust and sympathy between parent and child, the security and isolation from the dangers of the "adult" world, and an innocence of deceit.

Pallas' first combat and his death combine the *topoi* of erotic and heroic comings of age. Like Catullus' *virgo intacta* he leaves a haven, and Vergil's allusion presents the menace of the world outside Pallanteum as more than warfare: the operative threat is adulthood itself. Love and marriage should be a natural and appropriate end to childhood. For Catullus they lead instead to the failures and pain that torment him and that (he seems to insist) pervade adult life. Pallas should enter a heroic life that gives him identity and meaning, a life that is not available in the world of the epic.[57]

The simile is followed by a description of the laying out of Pallas' body.

55. See Kroll 1968 and Fordyce 1961, *ad loc.,* for parallels and comment.
56. Westendorp-Boerma 1958, especially 61–62, and Wigodsky 1972, 127 and 141.
57. For a discussion of some further possible epithalamic features (e.g., the twin shrouds as wedding veils) see Lyne 1989, 149–59.

Vergil models Pallas' shrouding on the Homeric burial of Hector (*Il.* 24.580–90), but again he gives this traditional material a more idiosyncratic spin:

> tum geminas vestis auroque ostroque rigentis
> extulit Aeneas, quas illi laeta laborum
> ipsa suis quondam manibus Sidonia Dido
> fecerat et tenui telas discreverat auro.

[Then Aeneas brought out twin cloaks stiff with gold and purple, which earlier Sidonian Dido had made for him, the work of her own hands, and she took pleasure in the work, parting the wefts with strands of gold.]

(*A.* 11.72–75)

Dido's gold and purple cloaks stand out sharply against the crude bier on which Pallas lies (*agresti stramine*, *A.* 11.67, and lines 64–66) and draw attention to the distance between Carthage, with all that it exemplifies, and the idealized simplicity of Pallas' life and realm. I have discussed in chapter 3 the other occurrences of Dido's gifts in the poem;[58] in this, their last appearance, Vergil takes us back to the passage in which Aeneas is told to leave Dido (*A.* 11.75 = *A.* 4.64), and thereby connects the earlier failure of Aeneas' love to the failure of his guardianship of Pallas:

> atque illi stellatus iaspide fulva
> ensis erat Tyrioque ardebat murice laena
> demissa ex umeris, dives quae munera Dido
> fecerat, et tenui telas discreverat auro.

[Aeneas' sword gleamed with yellow jasper and his cloak hung from his shoulder and shone like fire, dyed Tyrian purple: these wealthy Dido had made as gifts for him, parting the wefts with strands of gold.]

(*A.* 4.261–64)

One final passage belongs with these. We have seen earlier in this chapter that Vergil begins the episode in Pallanteum by equating childhood and traditional heroism. He concludes the episode with the same equation: Aeneas speaks over the corpse of Pallas.

> maestamque Evandri primus ad urbem
> mittatur Pallas, quem non virtutis egentem
> abstulit atra dies et funere mersit acerbo.

---

58. See "Dido" in chapter 3.

[Let Pallas first be sent to the grieving city of Evander, the boy whom, though wanting for no manly virtue, a black day has carried off and plunged into bitter death.]

(A. 11.26–28)

Non virtutis egentem is Ennian[59] and Vergil retains the elevated tones of his source, beginning the line with a series of spondees; the phrase suggests, as well, Heracles' hallmark virtue, *non . . . rationis egentem* (A. 8.299), all in all denoting a heroic character firmly placed in the heroic world. Vergil, however, follows the Ennian spondees with a line of dactyls from *Aeneid* 6 that describes infants' souls in the underworld:[60]

> Continuo auditae voces vagitus et ingens
> infantumque animae flentes, in limine primo
> quos dulcis vitae exsortis et ab ubere raptos
> abstulit atra dies et funere mersit acerbo.

[Immediately cries were heard and loud sobbing, the souls of infants as they wept, those whom, on the very threshold of life, a black day had carried off and plunged into bitter death, torn from their mothers' breast and deprived of sweet life.]

(A. 6.426–29)

Like the infants' souls, Pallas' entry into the world is cut short; his death, as Evander's only son, is the end of the *gens*, and it is perhaps the climax of Vergil's theme of lost progeny and lost posterity.[61]

INFELIX BALTEUS AND THE DEATH OF TURNUS

Any discussion of Pallas and Aeneas must consider the last scene of the poem, because of which the *Aeneid* is so often judged problematical: Pallas' death does not seem sufficient cause for the unsettling, even damning, final portrait of Aeneas yielding to *furor* and ignoring Anchises' command to the progenitors of empire, *Romane . . . parcere subiectis* [Ro-

---

59. Ennius frag. 605 Skutsch; see Servius *ad loc.*

60. Compare the simile of Euryalus' death, which combines a traditional Homeric image (a poppy bent down in the rain) with an image from Catullan love poetry; see "The Death of Euryalus" in chapter 3. For the juxtaposition of dactyls and spondees see Norden 1957, *ad A.* 6.429.

61. Latinus' family is equally threatened with extinction by the loss of an only son: *filius huic fato divum prolesque virilis / nulla fuit, primaque oriens erepta iuventa est* [Latinus had no son or male descendants, by heaven's will, though a son had died early in youth] (A. 7.50–51).

man . . . spare the conquered] (*A.* 6.853).[62] A few studies defend Vergil's conclusion by villainizing Turnus: they argue that his rashness and violence represent the sort of dangers that confront Augustan rule and the nascent Empire, and that Aeneas is the hero of the poem because he eliminates their threat. Such studies maintain, moreover, that vengeance is a moral and social obligation to Evander, and that Aeneas could not justly have acted other than he did; objections to the end of the poem are modern misreadings and critical anachronisms; to ancient readers Turnus deserves what he gets.[63]

Most critics (rightly, I think) remain unconvinced.[64] We should expect more balance in Aeneas, after all, the character with whom both Roman and Julio-Claudian history more or less begin. The broad lines of the narrative in *Aeneid* 10 plainly allude to the *furor* of Achilles after the death of Patroklos (*Il.* 18–22),[65] and the allusion effectively conveys the intensity of Aeneas' rage; it does not, however, adequately explain it, and in other respects the relationships between Aeneas and Pallas and between Achilles and Patroklos are hardly comparable. Furthermore, the calculus of retribution (Turnus' life for Pallas') in no way accounts for the suddenness and brutality of the poem's conclusion. We miss any satisfaction that accounts have been paid and debts settled, any sense of completeness or resolution. A recent book characterizes the uneasiness many have felt with the death of Turnus:

> . . . most readers find the violence and abruptness of the last scene disturbing; Aeneas' uncertainty seems to be not so much resolved as terminated. There is no sense of a high moral purpose attained, or a personal triumph; there is only grim reality—this terrible, final act of *pietas* required of the hero, which the poet, for reasons sufficient to his imagination, will not mitigate, will not explain away.[66]

I would like to consider for the next few pages what these "reasons sufficient to his imagination" might be, why Vergil allows no mitigation to restore his hero. Aeneas' rage in the final moments of the poem com-

---

62. Augustus' claim in *Res Gestae* 3 is relevant and often cited: *victorque omnibus veniam petentibus civibus peperci* [as victor I spared all citizens who asked for mercy]. For a discussion of the passage and its problems, and of Turnus' death generally, see Lyne 1983.

63. For a collection of these views see Galinsky 1988, and Willcock 1989: "The man [Turnus] is a thug."

64. Johnson's (1976, 114–34) discussion of the problem is particularly good; see further Lyne 1983 and Clausen 1987, 83–100.

65. See Knauer 1964, 417.

66. Clausen 1987, 100.

pels us to evaluate precisely his relationship with Pallas; by it Vergil is telling us something essential about the way his poem works and in turn, I suggest, about the workings of his contemporary Roman world. These conclusions will also shed some light on the immediate cause of Turnus' death, the *balteus* stripped from Pallas, engraved with images of the daughters of Danaus.

Pallas, Aeneas, and Heracles

The portrait of Aeneas at the end of the poem is disturbing, first, because it is so abrupt and, second, because in it we find degrees of grief and rage that seem inapposite. Critics resort increasingly to the notion that Pallas is a "surrogate son" in order to explain Aeneas' killing of Turnus and his plans for human sacrifice at Pallas' funeral:[67] both excesses arise out of a father's *(sic)* rage; in bereaved fathers any degree of anger is pardonable, even redeeming—one need look no further than Mezentius after Lausus' death.[68]

A father's love might indeed help excuse Aeneas' behavior; we can imagine how different the end of the poem would feel if Iulus' were the death Aeneas avenged or if Evander were Pallas' avenger. But the solution brings new problems: though Aeneas becomes Pallas' mentor and guardian (which can be a father-like relationship), why has Vergil omitted any convincing development of a paternal/filial bond, convincing enough, at least, to make the end of the poem predictable, if not inevitable? More difficult still, Vergil defines the bond between Aeneas and Pallas quite explicitly, and he avoids any suggestion that Aeneas feels himself or is felt to be in a father's role. In the crucial moment when Aeneas first hears that Pallas has been killed (A. 10.515–17, previously quoted) he responds with confusion, guilt, and an overwhelming sense of personal loss, but it is difficult not to feel that something is missing in this description: where is the love, paternal or otherwise, that the end of the poem implies Aeneas feels for his ward? He expresses shame and grieves at his (perceived) broken trust, *dextrae . . . datae* (517), and at the obligations of hospitality, *mensae* (516), that he feels he has betrayed, but nothing more;

---

67. A. 10.517–36.

68. Moskalew 1982, 178: "Whatever the obligation Aeneas incurred by allying himself with Evander and having Pallas entrusted to his care (cf. 8.514–17), it does not explain his extreme grief and rage at the death of Pallas. We are unprepared for this sudden emotional intensity, for Aeneas' reaction implies deep affection, if not love." Moskalew then goes on to describe Aeneas as surrogate father and Pallas as his "son."

these pledges and this alliance, Vergil stresses, cause Aeneas pain and produce his anger.

We find the same emphasis in another crucial moment. As Aeneas prepares to return Pallas' body to Evander, he begins his eulogy, again not with any mention of personal bereavement, but with guilt and remorse for his own bad faith:

> non haec Evandro de te promissa parenti
> discedens dederam, cum me complexus euntem
> mitteret in magnum imperium metuensque moneret
> acris esse viros, cum dura proelia gente.

[These were not the promises I made about you to your father, Evander, as I left, when embracing me he sent me forth on my quest for a great empire and fearfully warned that I would face a deadly enemy and do battle with a fierce people.]

(A. 11.45–48)

He dwells on the sorrow Evander will feel when he learns that his son has died (line 49) and on the consolation the father might take in his son's bravery; but Aeneas himself returns to his own failure, *haec mea magna fides?* [Is this my great pledge?] (A. 11.55), and laments Pallas' death as a loss to Iulus and to Rome: *ei mihi quantum / praesidium, Ausonia, et quantum tu perdis Iule* [what a defender and support you have lost, Italy, and you, Iulus] (A. 11.57–58). In these scenes Vergil forces us to notice the precise source of Aeneas' grief and fury: the responsibilities and violations of a social bond.

It is not enough to object that Aeneas is a character who rarely or imperfectly expresses emotion,[69] or that poetry has license to deal more in implication than in explication. Inference and suggestion should not replace what Vergil does say directly about Aeneas and Pallas. We face the same problems as previously occurred in Heracles' reaction to Pallas' imminent death (see "Heracles, Aeneas, and Augustus"); his tears are no less unexpected than Aeneas' rage and seem as incongruous. Some would make Heracles another "surrogate father" to explain the incongruity: the allusion to Zeus in *Iliad* 16 as he weeps at the death of

---

69. Lyne 1987, 75: "The implications of silence and inaction (Vergil's "negative" invention) must not be resisted. . . . Aeneas cannot, will not, anyway does not, react affectively at crucial moments in the main relationships of his life (with Creusa, Ascanius, Dido, Pallas). He seems to have the essential ability so to react, as his response to the dead Creusa and to the dead Dido demonstrates; but as these episodes also demonstrate, he seems prone to doing so, if at all, *too late*."

Sarpedon[70] and the words Vergil uses to introduce Jupiter's consolation, *tum genitor natum . . . adfatur* [then father addressed his son] (*A.* 10.466), suggest the theme of paternity and give the moment great pathos.[71] But these multiple suggestions of a father's love, and indeed, Vergil's invitation to infer here a father's love, deliberately lead nowhere. Pallas never feels himself to be Heracles' son: *hospitium* is the only focus of his appeal as he prays to his patron deity (*A.* 10.460–63, previously quoted). And though Heracles' tears recall those of Zeus for Sarpedon, they arise from a relationship that Vergil sketches sparingly, and then only by the same formal terms as in Aeneas' relationship to Pallas. Guest-friendship defines their bond, and Heracles' powerlessness to defend his host's son causes his (considerable) suffering.

Why does Vergil transform the climactic act of vengeance in the *Iliad* into a scene needing so much inference, and even, in fairness, so much special pleading? And why has Vergil grafted a celebrated example of a father's love for his son onto Pallas and Heracles, characters who have no discernible personal relationship at all? We can best answer these questions by abandoning the notions of "surrogate father" and "surrogate son" which allow us to mitigate what Vergil has not. Vergil raises these questions to direct us toward the cause of Aeneas' *furor* and Heracles' grief; in this cause lies his comment.

On the surface there is much here that seems familiar. Pallas and Aeneas are nominally related through Atlas and Mercury (*A.* 8.126–42), and Aeneas claims his kinship to Pallas in his final words in the poem, *tune hinc spoliis indute meorum eripiare mihi?* [Turnus, are you to be snatched away from me, wearing the spoils of my own?] (*A.* 12.947–48). Distant blood-ties through gods, though scarcely sufficient grounds for the intensity of Aeneas' emotion, are conventional features of epic poetry, no less than the bonds of epic guest-friendship. But Vergil weaves through these passages the terms of contemporary Roman political and social alliances, most obviously (though not exclusively) *amicitia: hospitium, fides, dextrae datae.*[72]

---

70. *A.* 10.464–65, previously quoted.

71. Lee 1980, 83: "So the surrogate father is partially consoled." By some accounts Heracles actually is Pallas' father, a tradition to which Vergil nods but that he then ignores: Servius *ad A.* 8.51 and D. H. *Ant.* 1.31.1 record a legend in which Pallas is the son of Heracles and Evander's daughter, Lavinia.

72. *Amicitia* is used nowhere in the *Aeneid* and requires some indulgence for its use here: whether, for example, Evander and Heracles share a bond of *amicitia* or something closer to a patron-client relationship is perhaps arguable but is not, I think, to the point.

Amicitia is one element of the network that binds together the ruling families and individuals in Roman political life. It could be an arrangement of expediency and self-interest, "a weapon of politics, not a sentiment based on congeniality,"[73] or it could entail more, a tie deep enough to survive crises and last decades, virtual kinship.[74] While recent studies have nuanced the precise limits and effects of such alliances,[75] their role in the intrigues and power struggles of the Roman aristocracy remains clear. To some extent the civil wars are orchestrated through them, at least, Horace suggests, in Pollio's estimate:

> Motum ex Metello consule civicum
> bellique causas et vitia et modos
> > ludumque Fortunae gravisque
> > > principum amicitias et arma
> nondum expiatis uncta cruoribus,
> periculosae plenum opus aleae,
> > tractas et incedis per ignis
> > > suppositos cineri doloso.

[You, Pollio, treat the upheaval of the state from the consulship of Metellus—the causes of the war, its evils, and the ways it came to pass; the twists of Fortune; the deadly friendships of the leading men, and their arms still slick with blood, blood even now unatoned for—a task full of perilous risk: you stride through hidden fires that still smolder beneath deceiving ash.]

(Odes 2.1.1–8)

The *Aeneid* (obviously) does not *precisely* replicate aspects of Italy in the first century: by using *hospitium, fides,* and *dextra datae* of Heracles and Aeneas' relationship to Pallas, Vergil summons up the general features of social and political connections in Republican Rome, as distinct from personal emotion. The bibliography on *amicitia* is vast; see, e.g., Syme 1939; Taylor 1949; and Brunt 1988, 352–81.

73. Syme 1939, 12; *The Roman Revolution* suggests how far these alliances go in explaining the configuration of the Roman aristocracy and the workings of government.

74. Brunt 1988, 356: " . . . *amicitia* often purports to describe sincere affection based on a community of tastes, feelings, and principles, and taking the form, where opportunity permits, of continuous and intimate association *(vetustas, familiaritas, consuetudo)."*

75. Brunt 1988, chapter 7, is a convincing challenge to the view that the machinations of the aristocracy alone, and their dependencies and mutual obligations, wholly account for the operations of the Roman state; cf. also Nicolet 1988, 6–7: "the attempt to explain almost everything in the political life of ancient Rome by the effects of kinship, marriages and factions—which were certainly important elements, but not exclusively so—is inevitably frustrated from time to time and leads in any case to a purely empirical and cynical view of events which takes too little account of the personal convictions, laws and morality of those concerned, not to mention their need for political support and pressure, weak though it may have been, of public opinion."

The chaos and terror in Rome during the years of the *Eclogues* and *Georgics* (42–27 B.C.) give way gradually to order under the principate. Caesar's assassins and the triumvirate (Octavian's enemies and rivals) are brought to decisive, violent ends; with them disappear some of the arbitrary uses of power in Rome and the threats of unforeseeable catastrophe. Throughout these times of destruction and rebuilding, nevertheless, the traditional means of acquiring and maintaining power remain:

> in . . . the Principate . . . the game of politics is played in the same arena as before; the competitors for power and wealth require the same weapons, namely *amicitia*, the dynastic marriage and the financial subsidy.[76]

It is possible, therefore (though arguably reductive), to write the fortunes of Rome in the late Republic—the deaths of Cicero and Antony, the machinations of Agrippa and of Livia, and especially Augustus' struggle to confirm an heir—as the effects of these coalitions and allegiances, as the history of their victims and beneficiaries. And it is equally clear why Vergil has elevated them to such prominence in his poem.

To review the argument to this point: in these key scenes Vergil invests his mythical figures with the ramifications of social and political bonds in contemporary Rome and so produces a striking metamorphosis. It is no surprise that *amicitia* and social alliances produce emotion, or that a mentor (whom we have grown accustomed to call a "surrogate father") can feel deeply for his ward: such relationships are in no sense abstractions. But it is surprising that even as Vergil faithfully preserves the central scenes and deepest passions of the *Iliad,* he gives his characters new (and Roman) motives and their passions a different (and equally Roman) source: Achilles' rage at Patroklos' death becomes in the *Aeneid* a reaction caused by social obligation and distant kinship; Zeus' grief for his son Sarpedon glosses the consequences and costs of *hospitium* and *fides*. Vergil has moved his spotlight from the fierce loyalties and excesses of love, and onto the equally (implicitly) fierce loyalties and excesses of social alliances: *gravis . . . principum amicitias*. Vergil leaves us with images of Heracles in tears and Aeneas raging and unredeemed, but for reasons that are clear only with a second, deeper look, and only after the uncomfortable sense that the familiar motives and characters in earlier poetry no longer tell us how this world works: in the *Aeneid,* as in Vergil's own day, political vengeance and social alliances are the new and fundamental passions, the passions of empire; as the poem evolves they come to supplant love as the source of paralyzing grief and uncontrolled violence.

---

76. Syme 1939, 376.

Dido and Amata

This interpretation is confirmed by other characters and their relationships elsewhere in the poem. Vergil's transmutation of the effects of personal emotion and familial love to the social and political sphere in the episode of Dido has already been noted: Aeneas' abandonment of her presents graphically how love is subverted by the demands of statehood and fate:[77]

> sed nunc Italiam magnam Gryneus Apollo,
> Italiam Lyciae iussere capessere sortes;
> hic amor, hic patria est.

[But now Grynean Apollo, the oracle of Lycia, bids me to seek Italy, great Italy; there is my love, there my nation.]

(*A.* 4.345–47)

The irony of *amor* in its new incarnation ("Italiam") points to this subversion, further strengthened by another detail. Aeneas is directed to his new goal by *Gryneus Apollo,* a surprisingly arcane choice of prophetic seats. In Latin poetry the Grynean grove is named only here and in the sixth *Eclogue,* where it is the subject of the verses that Gallus will write when he joins those who have inherited Hesiod's pipes:[78]

> his tibi Grynei nemoris dicatur origo,
> ne quis sit lucus quo se plus iactet Apollo.

[With these pipes sing the origins of the Grynean grove, that there be no grove in which Apollo takes greater pride.]

(*Ecl.* 6.72–73)

Too little remains of Gallus' poetry to explain confidently the grove's inclusion here, but we can perhaps offer a guess in light of the themes under discussion. The topic that places Gallus in the company of Hesiod, perhaps of Orpheus, but most of all in the Alexandrian movement in Rome, resurfaces in the *Aeneid* linked to a heroic character rejecting love and engaging in the work of epic. Aeneas turns from love, turns, in effect, toward the world of *reges et proelia,* topics specifically prohibited by Apollo at the start of the sixth *Eclogue* (lines 3–5)—epic deeds, moreover,

---

77. See "Loss and the Domestic World" in this chapter.

78. Presumably these verses had already been written by Gallus, most likely under Parthenius' influence, and were translated from, or at least modeled on, Euphorion; see Servius *ad loc.* and Ross 1975, 79–80 and 86–87.

that Aeneas now calls *amor*. As Vergil systematically recasts conventional love to fit the character of the poem, so the spirit and material of Gallus' poetry—love elegies, as seems likely, on Lycoris, and written according to Alexandrian *dicta*[79]—are appropriated to the themes of epic and the concerns of empire.

Amata and Turnus provide a more elaborate example of this changed nature of love, a change that becomes a constant theme in the second half of the *Aeneid*.[80] Dido has an analogue in Amata, wife of Latinus: like Dido she is inflamed by a god (*A.* 7.341–48), driven through the city like a bacchant (*A.* 7.385–405), and, finally, when it is clear that Turnus is lost, kills herself (*A.* 12.596–603). She suggests lovers in tragedy and romance, as well as Dido, and the symptoms of fatal infatuation seem unmistakable, but with whom or with what is her infatuation? Some critics have taken Vergil's suggestions of lovelorn heroines literally: Amata is inspired by Allecto according to certain erotic predilections she unconsciously has; Phaedra-like, she already loves her daughter's husband-to-be, and her passion is merely unleashed, not implanted, by Allecto.[81]

But what would Vergil's point be? Is it an observation about a certain kind of erotic pathology, exotic and therefore interesting? Or can it be generalized to suggest that all or most mothers will feel some attraction for their future sons-in-law? Though the broad outlines of the narrative suggest erotic love, the details do not. Amata pleads with Latinus as her madness begins: *mollius et solito matrum de more locuta est* [She spoke soothingly, in the usual way of mothers] (*A.* 7.357); as Allecto's poison takes full effect Amata goes off to the woods with a collection of women in a makeshift *thiasos*, and declares that only Bacchus is worthy of her daughter; her raging determination for the marriage grows, and she looks to the other Latin mothers for support:

> ipsa inter medias flagrantem fervida pinum
> sustinet ac natae Turnique canit hymenaeos
> sanguineam torquens aciem, torvumque repente
> clamat: 'io matres, audite, ubi quaeque, Latinae:
> si qua piis animis manet infelicis Amatae
> gratia, si iuris materni cura remordet,

---

79. See Ross 1975, especially chapter 3; on Gallus as a writer of epyllia see Weber 1978.

80. Cf. the role of Venus: in the opening books she is mother and grandmother, caring for her family; she evolves in the second half of the poem to become a war goddess, bringing arms to Aeneas amid images of fire and blood; cf. Wlosok 1967.

81. See Zarker 1969 and Lyne 1987, 116–17.

solvite crinalis vittas, capite orgia mecum.'
talem inter silvas, inter deserta ferarum
reginam Allecto stimulis agit undique Bacchi.

[In the midst of the women Amata, herself inflamed, raises a burning
torch and sings the wedding hymn for Turnus and her daughter, rolling
bloodshot eyes, and suddenly calling wildly: "Hear me Latin mothers,
all of you everywhere: if any affection still remains in your pious hearts
for poor Amata, if any care for the rights due a mother concerns you,
loosen your headbands, join me in the revels." Thus Allecto harried the
queen from every side with the goads of Bacchus, through the woods,
among the lairs of wild beasts.]

(A. 7.397–405)

If there is erotic desire for Turnus here, it seems well hidden: Amata
holds a mock wedding for her daughter and Turnus, complete with
torches and epithalamion, and she invokes her rights as mother of the
bride (lines 401–3). She walks, so to speak, in Phaedra's robes on Dido's
stage, all the machinery of allusion and representation appropriate to a
character in hopeless and unlawful love, and yet strangely, her passion
and fury seem to focus not on any desire for Turnus himself but on the
desire that her daughter marry her nephew—*furor* created by and fueled
by a rather commonplace social and political arrangement. She next appears in Book 12 before Turnus' duel with Aeneas and her words there
convey the same rage at the possibility of a Trojan son-in-law. Amata begs
Turnus not to fight Aeneas:

Turne, per has ego te lacrimas, per si quis Amatae
tangit honos animum (spes tu nunc una, senectae
tu requies miserae, decus imperiumque Latini
te penes, in te omnis domus inclinata recumbit.)
unum oro: desiste manum committere Teucris.
qui te cumque manent isto certamine casus
et me, Turne, manent; simul haec invisa relinquam
lumina nec generum Aenean captiva videbo.

[Turnus, I beg you by these tears, by any esteem you may hold in your
heart for Amata (for you now are my one hope, you are my only solace
for wretched old age, in you reside the glory and power of Latinus, upon
you the declining fortunes of our whole house depend). I ask only one
thing: avoid single combat with the Trojans: whatever fate befalls you in
that battle will befall me also; I will leave this hated life when you do:
never as a captive will I accept Aeneas for a son.]

(A. 12.56–63)

Impassioned and fierce language, and commentators (beginning in antiquity) have expressed some surprise at the violence of Amata's resolve,[82] but how erotic are her words?

Though there are general suggestions of Andromache's plea to Hector in *Iliad* 6, the scene as a whole and Amata's words in particular are as close or closer to Hecuba's, the mother of Hector, before her son's last duel with Achilles in *Iliad* 22.[83] Lines 57–58, *spes tu nunc una, senectae / tu requies miserae,* virtually repeat Euryalus' mother's lament at her son's death in *Aeneid* 9, *senectae sera meae requies* (481–82), and are not far from Evander's warnings to his son Pallas in Book 8, *mea sola et sera voluptas* (581; cf. 578–84). All are peculiar reminiscences if Vergil intends to suggest in Amata overwhelming sexual desire.

It is an undeniably odd picture: a mother's interest in a contractual marriage—and merely contractual, for the possibility that Lavinia and Turnus are in love is beside any point Amata makes—pursued, under Allecto's influence, with the frenzy and fatal desperation of a scorned lover. One could assume hidden pathology: that Amata feels desires for Turnus that she (perhaps understandably) can't quite acknowledge, but that (less understandably) Vergil leaves unconnected to the surrounding narrative—an explosive theme introduced only to be orphaned in an otherwise tight network of associations. The picture is less odd once we recognize that beneath her bacchic ravings and suggestions of "Asian" barbarity Amata acts in a familiar capacity: Roman *matronae,* within and outside their own families, took part in negotiating marriages, and the role formed an important basis of their domestic authority and public ambitions.[84] Allecto has not displaced Amata's maternal prerogatives with incestuous desire; she has given Amata's rights (*iuris materni, A.* 12.402) murderous intensity. This commonplace social and familial bond (an arranged marriage) inflames and destroys Amata along with those around her; it is a bond that imitates, but only in intensity and effect, the symptoms of erotic love.

The more we apply what we know of Roman social history to this portrait, the more striking it becomes, the more clearly formed to the mate-

82. Servius Danielis *ad A.* 12.63: *mire et fidem suam et studium circa Turnum expressit* [she expressed her devotion to Turnus and her affection for him in an extraordinary way].

83. Knauer 1964, 426.

84. The evidence for matrons' involvement in marriage arrangements is sketchy but seems unambiguous; see Phillips 1978; Dixon 1985, 215–28; and Treggiari 1991, 126–38. I am indebted to Bettini (1991, especially 67–99) for his discussion of Amata.

rial of Vergil's contemporary world. Dynastic marriages are a cornerstone of the Roman aristocracy, the link by which leading families attempt (often in vain) to end rivalries and heal factions: in 40 B.C. the marriage of Octavia and Antony is intended to stabilize the Peace of Brundisium; Octavian's three marriages in seven years are a map of his political affiliations and aspirations.[85] Especially in the late Republic and under the Julio-Claudians, marriages consistently attend the shifts of power and influence.[86] Amata is not, of course, another Livia, a restless Machiavellian gathering personal and political authority; Vergil focuses on dynastic marriages themselves, and he takes for his themes their place at the pressure points of Roman life and their volatility. In creating Amata Vergil moves beyond the usual poetic psychologies of hopeless love, and he converts the *topoi* and conceits of erotic inspiration and tragic infatuation to a new purpose. "Demonic possession," conformed to the Roman landscape of the last half of the *Aeneid*, is no longer an inspired sexual passion that overwhelms law, piety, and reason; Allecto's furies invade and rend where the social fabric (in Vergil's Rome) is most at risk, and they produce starkly realistic images of political discord: could mere love or sexual desire, after all, produce the fury and tragedies that consume Rome at the end of the Republic, or could they account for the fires of the civil wars that, Horace reminds us, still smolder beneath deceiving ash?

Through Aeneas, Heracles, and Amata, Vergil aims, as he does throughout the *Aeneid*, to portray and examine his contemporary world and its recent history. Though the scenes and figures of earlier poets are his inevitable models, they are given Roman hearts and minds, drawn from the street, the forum, the senate house. It is a monumental achievement, but no more than Vergil had claimed for the *Aeneid* a decade earlier. We can return again to the proem of the third *Georgic* and the weariness registered there with Alexandrian themes, with the glut of *pathemata*, erotic and heroic, that had come to fill the center of the literary world:

85. Octavian's first marriage to Antony's stepdaughter, Claudia, marks his reconciliation with Antony and is a seal on the triumvirate; next, as an overture to Sextus Pompeius, he marries Scribonia, Pompeius' kinswoman; two years later he divorces her—on the day she gives birth to Julia, his only child—to marry Livia. Syme 1939, 378: "The schemes devised by Augustus in the ramification of family alliances were formidable and fantastic. He neglected no relative, however obscure, however distant, no tie whatever of marriage—or of friendship retained after divorce."

86. Syme 1939, 12: "Marriage with a well-connected heiress . . . became an act of policy and an alliance of powers, more important than a magistracy, more binding than any compact or oath or interest." Brunt (1988, 453–55) details the failure of such marriages to produce lasting amity. See further Corbier 1991 and Treggiari 1991, 478–82.

cetera, quae vacuas tenuissent carmine mentes,
omnia iam vulgata: quis aut Eurysthea durum
aut inlaudati nescit Busiridis aras?
cui non dictus Hylas puer et Latonia Delos
Hippodameque umeroque Pelops insignis eburno,
acer equis?

[Other themes, which might have entertained idle minds with song, are
all now tired and worn: who has not heard about harsh Eurystheus or
the altars of cursed Busiris? By whom has the boy Hylas not been sung,
and Latonian Delos, and Hippodamia and Pelops, famed for his ivory
shoulder, swift with horses?]

(G. 3.3–8)

Vergil's solution in the *Aeneid* to the problem of hackneyed themes and
stock characters was not greater erudition and more determined obscu-
rity. He turns to the principles (without the themes) of Callimachus and
of the Alexandrians, and to Homer, the poet perhaps most assiduously
imitated, but profoundly transforms both. Homeric causation and characterization, and the intense scrutiny of exotic love and personal emotion
in Alexandrian poetry (however subtle and impressive in their own
right), could not possibly comprehend the historical and national questions that occupy Romans so persistently as the civil wars end, as Octavian becomes Augustus, and as the Republic becomes the Empire. In
transforming Achilles, Zeus, or Phaedra, Vergil has not drained the
power from his Greek models, rendering them lifeless and bloodless; they
move and affect us, as no mere replications could, by absorbing and pro-
jecting his fellow Romans' greatest passions and vulnerabilities.

The Daughters of Danaus

To return to the final scene of the poem: Turnus pleads for his life and
almost succeeds; Aeneas, about to drop his sword and to spare his enemy,
remembers Pallas and with renewed fury (*furiis accensus et ira terribilis, A.*
12.946–47) avenges the boy he has failed to protect: *Pallas te hoc vulnere,
Pallas / immolat et poenam scelerato ex sanguine sumit* [Pallas gives you this
wound, Turnus, Pallas exacts payment from your criminal blood] (*A.*
12.948–49]. The immediate cause for Aeneas' *furor* is the *balteus* that Turnus stripped from Pallas' corpse:

et laevo pressit pede talia fatus
exanimem rapiens immania pondera baltei

> impressumque nefas: una sub nocte iugali
> caesa manus iuvenum foede thalamique cruenti,
> quae Clonus Eurytides multo caelaverat auro.

[Thus he spoke, and held down the lifeless body with his foot, tearing away the heavy sword-belt carved with the infamous deed: the band of men, slaughtered together on their wedding night, foully slaughtered, and the bloody bridal chambers, which Clonus, son of Eurytus, had engraved there with much gold.]

(*A.* 10.495–99)

Vergil refers elliptically to the story of the Danaids, the fifty daughters of Danaus who are compelled to marry their cousins, the fifty sons of Aegyptus. By their father's orders they conceal weapons on their wedding night and commit an act of vengeance: Danaus has been driven from his homeland by Aegyptus, his brother and rival, and out of spite he instructs his daughters to kill their new husbands while they sleep. For their crime they are condemned to spend eternity in the underworld carrying water in broken jars. Versions of the story exist in which a single daughter refuses her father's commands and spares her husband; Horace (*Odes* 2.14) and the (pseudo-)Ovidian *Heroides* 14 have interest only in the pious daughter and the redemptive power of love. Vergil's focus is clearly different: there is no mention of the exceptional daughter, no mythographer's interest in exotic punishments, only the betrayed bridegrooms, the bloody bridal chambers.

Two interpretations have appeared that deserve mention. The first, mainly archaeological, consists of tantalizing correspondences but ultimately contributes more problems than solutions. Paul Zanker and, independently, Barbara Kellum,[87] understand Vergil's scene as a compliment to Augustus, connecting the Danaids on Pallas' belt with those featured on the temple of Palatine Apollo, dedicated by Augustus in 28 B.C. According to Propertius (2.31) the temple had for its portico columns of Danaids in yellow marble, veined, appropriately, with blood red; a scholiast to Persius (though he is the only source) adds that the bridegrooms, the sons of Aegyptus, were represented by fifty equestrian statues. The temple avoids the usual depiction of the Danaids in art, that is, as water carriers in the underworld;[88] we find, by contrast, the crime in

---

87. See Kellum 1981, chapter 2, and Zanker 1983.

88. Also their usual presentation in literature: Horace *Odes* 3.11.23–24, Tibullus 1.3.79–81, and Ovid *Met.* 4.462–63 all include the Danaids in catalogs of the impious in

progress,[89] an almost unique presentation—Vergil is the other important exception. Zanker and Kellum argue that the statues symbolize fratricide and civil war, and Augustus' triumph, with the aid of Apollo, over these forces.[90] Vergil, therefore, under the influence of the sculptural program, aligns Turnus with the war and discord that the Danaids represent, and Aeneas (i.e., Augustus) with the restoration of order and the winning of peace.[91]

It is difficult to imagine that Vergil could have produced his passage with no thought of the temple, particularly one that attracted so much attention from his literary contemporaries. But it is equally difficult, and even impossible, to determine the relationship between the text and the building. However transparent the "message" of the sculptural program might be, we may obviously not simply assume that Vergil felt inclined or compelled to promote its views. At the very least, does the final portrait of Aeneas killing Turnus oppose impiety and piety so neatly? It is Aeneas who is consumed with fury and madness, while Turnus is the suppliant victim. And if the Danaids, embodying violence and destruction, gloss Turnus while he wears their image, how do we explain their significance while Pallas wears the belt? Whatever the correct interpretation of the temple's program, Vergil's passage seems more complex than these straightforward ethical alignments permit. Above all, the *Aeneid* must be understood independently before we can consider Vergil's relationship to Augustus' more overt acts of self-promotion—if that in fact is what the temple is.

By a different interpretation, G. B. Conte has argued that the image on the *balteus* represents the theme of *mors immatura*, young men killed before their time; the deaths of the bridegrooms repeat Pallas' own untimely death, as well as the deaths of Euryalus, Lausus, and others. The Danaids (though more exactly, the sons of Aegyptus) are a blend of two *topoi*, youths who die before marriage (ἄγαμοι), and youths killed before

---

the underworld, together with Ixion, Tityos, and Tantalus. Cf. Hyg. *Fab.* 31.10 and see Bömer 1976, II. 158–59.

89. Ovid (*Tristia* 3.1) says that Danaus' statue stood among his daughters' with sword drawn, urging them to their crime.

90. Kellum 1981, 66–67, and Zanker 1983, 30: "Die beiden [Antony and Cleopatra] hatten unter Bruch der Verträge hinterhältig das Verderben für Rom und Italien vorbereitet. Vor dem schrecklichen Ende hatte Octavian mit Hilfe Apollons das Land gerettet."

91. Kellum 1981, 66–67: "[Aeneas] kills one embodiment of *furor impius,* who was at that time wearing a representation of another. . . . It was exactly this kind of madness that Octavian claimed to have imprisoned with his victory over Antony and Cleopatra."

their time (ἄωροι), each as different sides of the same coin: for the sons of Aegyptus death comes too soon and before their wedding day, just as death comes for Pallas.[92] This interpretation touches on themes that have been important throughout the *Aeneid* and indicates a productive direction an interpretation might take; still, I believe we can press the details of the passage further.

How has Vergil gotten us to this point? What has prepared us for the Danaids here, and why has Vergil chosen this myth for the climactic image in the final moments of the poem?[93] The preceding discussions of Catullus suggest one direction in which answers might lie.

Vergil emphasizes not the brides' impiety or the youth of the bridegrooms (Conte's ἄγαμοι is a bit inexact) but the circumstances of the deaths, the wedding night, and the bridal chambers covered in blood. I have already discussed Vergil's treatment of marriage and its images, an essentially Catullan view. Pallas and then Turnus wear an image of a wedding night into battle, a perverse wedding night though it may be: Vergil leaves us with a picture that comprehends images that have come before but that also exceeds them, and he presents the end of innocence at its most stark and most brutal, the most extreme implication of this marriage imagery. The myth does not describe a reckless crime of passion; these are calculated murders to exact vengeance, Danaus' upon his brother Aegyptus. The wedding night of the Danaids suggests a world in which the brides are not simply (as in Catullus' similes) figures of transient and passing innocence; in the final books of the *Aeneid* innocence is dead, and the brides have become instruments in a violent stratagem, an image of political fury and political deaths. Vergil, by linking these themes to Aeneas' vengeance upon Turnus, to his "final act of *pietas*," has made this scene an emblem of the cardinal threat facing the future Roman state.

Catullus and Vergil

In the preceding chapters I have used specific passages and images to argue for Vergil's reading (or perhaps one of his readings) of Catullus' poetry. We are in a position now to consider a different sort of reference,

92. Conte 1986, 190–92.
93. A detail so significantly placed and so brief and enigmatic strongly suggests an allusion and the possibility that Vergil refers us to some text (now lost) that would make clear what now seems obscure and elusive.

one that, while at least as important, is purely conceptual—a borrowing of and alluding to a set of ideas rather than to words or passages.

Vergil is obviously not the first to use love metaphorically, nor is the metaphor itself rare. Applying the imagery and vocabulary of love as he does (whether erotic or familial) to the intensity and *furor* of political and social relations is thoroughgoing and systematic in the *Aeneid* and it cannot be understood as an accident of shared language or as a commonplace conceit. The Roman author before Vergil who conflates love with politics so systematically is Catullus: in his epigrams (69–116) Catullus appropriates a whole set of (nearly) technical terms—*fides, officium, benevolentia, gratia*—to describe his love affair with Lesbia, and the central metaphor for his experience with her becomes that of a political alliance, *amicitia*.[94] It is not that these words typically used for Roman social and political bonds provide Catullus with original or (least of all) convenient figures for the vagaries of his romance: *dilexi tum te ... pater ut gnatos diligit et generos* [I loved you then, Lesbia ... as a father loves his sons and sons-in-law] (72.3–4) cannot be anyone's idea of an effective erotic appeal. The metaphor begins to supplant the affair and Lesbia herself (whatever actual relationship or lover lies behind them): "Lesbia ... has become only a shadow representing the iniquities of the present, and the affair itself is now a moving and affective synonym for betrayal of trust, for a general dissolution of human values."[95]

We should consider the possibility that Vergil, who took so much else from Catullus, also absorbed and appropriated his predecessor's elaborate analogy between a love affair and Roman political culture, between the inevitable failure of love, that is, and the failure of the trust and mutual good faith that once bound together Rome—an idealized Rome, of course, in an idealized past. Vergil similarly uses erotic images to describe Amata and her wrath in an essentially social contract; she is inspired by the gods, as if another Dido or Medea, and driven to suicide by a divinely induced obsession that her daughter marry Turnus. Though Aeneas and Heracles suffer at Pallas' death as if at the death of their own child (so the language and allusions suggest), Vergil suppresses or mutes details that might convincingly present so close a bond, until the suggestions of "fathers and sons" seem unsatisfying and insufficient. As love (of any sort) becomes increasingly figurative and metaphoric, the world of the poem seems emptier, its characters increasingly desolate, and the

---

94. See Ross 1969, 80–93, and 1975, 1–17.
95. Ross 1975, 14.

causes for their behavior less comprehensibly "psychological." Apollo-nius' Eros and Medea (*Argo.* 3.114–50 and 751–65) or Theocritus' Si-maetha (*Idyll* 2, quoted in chapter 1), were obviously available to Vergil, and he models characters on them (e.g., Cupid and Dido) where they suit his needs; in these final books of the poem Vergil chooses instead to de-scribe different impulses and motives in order to depict a perhaps more real and more Roman view of life. The *Aeneid* is less a poem about love, in the end, than about the fierceness of social and political commitments and the agony and unrestrained violence that their obligations produce.

CHAPTER V

Iulus

The *Aeneid* is suffused with a sense of faded glory: in place of Homeric or Alexandrian young queens and brides we find a lonely widow in mid-life, and an aging Andromache waiting, sibyl-like, to die; some heroes (Diomedes and Antenor) have done all and seen all and finally escaped;[1] for Aeneas and others there is exhaustion but no relief—with *arma virumque* they must begin again, not (with any certainty) for the last time.

This version of the Roman past surely comments on Vergil's present. Since the *Aeneid* purports to be an etiology for the strengths and failures of Rome in Vergil's own day, Aeneas and Augustus stand at parallel moments in history, each looking on a past and a present of warfare and suffering, and each looking ahead, always ahead, to the eventual peace that their struggles will earn.[2]

In this equation (and only in this equation) Iulus emerges as the most important character in the poem, the crucial link between present and future. He appears in eleven books of the *Aeneid*, a peripheral figure with only occasional effect on the narrative and with little characterization, a sketch rather than a portrait of the only real child in the poem. Ascanius' age is notoriously difficult to fix; no age could easily suit both the little boy in Carthage, held and caressed in Dido's lap, and the killer of Remulus in Book 9, shown over a lapse in real time of (at most) a few months.[3]

This awkwardness should direct our attention to Iulus' thematic role in the poem. His development falls into three distinct movements. In the first four books (approximately)[4] he is a beautiful child who appears

---

1. Antenor finds a new home at Padua, *A.* 1.242–49, finally at rest, *nunc placida compostus pace quiescat* [he is settled now in gentle peace] (line 249); cf. Diomedes' account of Troy and his subsequent *labores*, *A.* 11.252–93.

2. Zetzel (1989, 272) discussing the underworld in Book 6: "the underworld is not frozen in the narrative time of the *Aeneid* or of myth. Its burden is historical, and is directed to the concerns of the Augustan age."

3. See Pease 1935, *ad A.* 4.84, for the main views and discussion.

4. Iulus hunts in Book 4, but he merely rides along, hoping to see wild boars or lions—enthusiasm that marks him as all the more childlike.

chiefly in the company of women as a real or surrogate son, to Creusa, to Andromache, and to Dido. In Books 5–8 he appears in "training" episodes, the hunts and war games that typically prepare *pueri* for adulthood. In the final third of the poem he is a child in the adult world, associated with increasing intimations that he has inherited ancestral afflictions: besieged in a walled camp (called *Troia, A.* 10.378), and associated (whether accurately or not) with the failures of his *gens*.[5] He commits his first adult deed, the killing of Remulus, only to be pulled back by Apollo and told, in effect, to remain a child: *cetera parce, puer, bello* [from here on, boy, refrain from further battle] (*A.* 9.656).

The character and qualities of Aeneas' heir will necessarily define the new Rome that will grow from the ruins of old Troy. Iulus is Rome's hope and the prophetic focus of the *Aeneid;* can Rome, through him, escape its past and make its ideals of innocence and virtue real? Moreover, the world of the epic destroys childhood and its cultural equivalents (heroic innocence, the primitive *virtus* of an idealized past), and Ascanius will live; how is the child who survives changed?

The poem's answers are deliberately unclear. Tradition gives Ascanius a much greater role than Vergil does in the Latin war and in the establishment of the Trojan settlement;[6] in the *Aeneid* he is brought to the verge of adulthood but goes no further, in order that his nature and the values he embodies be left unrealized. Ascanius' oddly lingering childhood reflects Vergil's uncertainty, about Augustus, about the subsidence of wars, about the emergence of real peace, and it is required by two incompatible demands: on the one hand Ascanius must be Rome's hope, the *spes gentis,* who, Apollo claims, will finally escape the past: *iure omnia bella / gente sub Assaraci fato ventura resident, / nec te Troia capit* [all wars fated to come will justly end under Assaracus' descendants; Troy no longer holds you] (*A.* 9.642–44); on the other hand he is a character increasingly (and seemingly inevitably) caught in the poem's labyrinth of deceptions and failure. We are faced in the end with the confident pronouncements of Rome's freedom from Troy and from the patterns of history, and with the stages of Iulus' evolution, which cumulatively suggest that no escape is possible.

5. Turnus (*A.* 9.135–55) makes explicit the obvious similarities between Trojans past and present.

6. Servius (*ad A.* 1.267, 4.620, 9.745) cites different accounts of Ascanius' role in the war and in the new Trojan community. According to Cato, the extant source before Vergil, Ascanius survives his father and kills Mezentius (*Origines* frag. 9); see Heinze 1915, 172.

ASCANIUS IN CARTHAGE

Cupid's deception of Dido diverges from that of Vergil's model in the *Argonautica*, Eros' of Medea (3.111–66 and 275–98), and from these differences emerge the central themes of the *Aeneid*. Vergil departs from the simple Hellenistic preoccupation with the power of love and the pathology of fatal infatuation and exploits instead the power of a less conventional desire: Dido is a mature woman and is childless, *infelix*;[7] Cupid, in the form of young Ascanius, is a particularly cruel appeal to her loneliness and desire to have a child. Childhood and even the desire for children become implicated in the epic world's tendency to corrupt and destroy.

Venus' deception is a conflict of private interests, *curae*, that embroil all characters, leaving only Iulus untouched. We find here a darker tone than the comic charm of Apollonius' episode, and the same elements—darkness, fire, betrayal—that describe the fall of Troy.[8] Like other deceptions we have seen, this occurs by night, *tu faciem illius noctem non amplius unam / falle dolo* [wear his appearance for one night only, as a trick] (*A.* 1.683–84), the time when danger is always greatest: *urit atrox Iuno et sub noctem cura recursat* [Fierce Juno burned, and at night her rage returned] (*A.* 1.662). The common etymology, *urit . . . cura recursat* (*cura = quod cor urit*),[9]

---

7. Pease 1935, *ad A.* 4.68; cf. Anna's response to Dido's guilty confession of love:

> o luce magis dilecta sorori,
> solane perpetua maerens carpere iuventa
> nec dulcis natos Veneris nec praemia noris?

> [Sister, dearer to me than life itself, will you spend your life alone,
> in mourning, and never know the sweetness of children nor love's rewards?]
> (*A.* 4.31–33)

In *Aeneid* 6 *infelix* is similarly used of Brutus, who loses his sons (see "Loss and the Domestic World" in chapter 4). For this sense of the word in different contexts see Boyd 1983.

8. See "Troy and Childhood" in chapter 3.

9. See Varro (*L.L.* 6.46): *cura, quod cor urat* (quoted by Servius, *ad A.* 4.1). Vergil uses his own *schema etymologicum*, *cura* in *recursat*, all three times that *recurso* appears:

> At regina gravi iamdudum saucia *cura*
> vulnus alit venis et caeco carpitur igni.
> multa viri virtus animo multusque *recursat*
> gentis honos.
> (*A.* 4.1–4)

and *et mihi curae / saepe tuo dulci tristes ex ore recursent* (*A.* 12.801–2).

establishes fire as the controlling image of the passage, and Juno's wrath and Venus' deception of Dido are described by images of burning. Cupid will delude Dido and ring her with flames (*capere ante dolis et cingere flamma / reginam meditor*, A. 1.673–74), and he inspires her with fire and poison (*occultum inspires ignem fallasque veneno*, A. 1.688), until the queen burns (*ardescit*, A. 1.713).

Although Venus' concern for Ascanius is maternal, *mea maxima cura* (A. 1.678),[10] *cura* here suggests fire and burning by the insistent etymologies of the previous lines. Every interest in the scene is defined as a fire that consumes and compels characters to violent action. Juno's hatred and Cupid's *eros* are emotions predictably described as fire; to describe Venus' maternal care by the same imagery is striking, another assertion that the same intensity and ferocity affect all relationships and all sympathies in the poem.[11] In the *Aeneid, curae* of every kind cause devastations: childhood itself is a deception, and love for children becomes a consuming and fatal desire:

> haec oculis, haec pectore toto
> haeret et interdum gremio fovet inscia Dido
> insidat quantus miserae deus.

[Dido drank in all this with her eyes, with her whole breast, and fondled the boy in her lap, all the while unaware how powerful a god was stealing deep into her heart.]

(*A.* 1.717–19)

Venus' abduction of Iulus is the first of many attempts in the poem to keep him separate from and unaffected by the character of Aeneas' world. Iulus must be replaced by Cupid and know nothing about the trick: *ne qua scire dolos . . . possit* (A. 1.682). He has refuge in fragrant groves and shade:

> at Venus Ascanio placidam per membra quietem
> inrigat, et fotum gremio dea tollit in altos
> Idaliae lucos, ubi mollis amaracus illum
> floribus et dulci aspirans complectitur umbra.

[But Venus sent soothing sleep through Ascanius' limbs and, caressing

---

10. Cf. the same phrase, *tua maxima cura*, of Cyrene's concern for her son Aristaeus (G. 4.354).

11. See, for example, "Pallas, Aeneas, and Heracles" and "Dido and Amata" in chapter 4.

him in her lap, carried him to the high Idalian groves, where the blooms
of fragrant marjoram enfolded him in their flowers and sweet shade.]

(*A.* 1.691–94)

The beauty and security of the pastoral sanctuary (Norden calls this passage "one of the most tender scenes in the poem")[12] are in contrast to the
surrounding fire and violence, an idyllic landscape, furthermore, with
associations to the imagery of childhood in Catullus.[13] That such beauty
and ease (and such a portrait of childhood) exist only in contrast to and
isolation from the epic's realities implicitly threatens Ascanius' future.
Given the world of the *Aeneid* and its tendency to absorb and transform
(for ill) even the most benign affections and values, when and how will
Iulus be integrated into the poem and how will the *spes gentis* avoid the
same error and guilt by association?

From the beginning of the poem, then, childhood and the isolated
shade of pastoral are aligned against the qualities of adulthood—*dolus,*
eros, and *dolor*—which are defined by metaphors of fire and heat.

Parvulus Aeneas

At the height of Dido's rage at Aeneas' departure she regrets that she has
no child by him:

> saltem si qua mihi de te suscepta fuisset
> ante fugam suboles, si quis mihi parvulus aula
> luderet Aeneas, qui te tamen ore referret,
> non equidem omnino capta ac deserta viderer.

[If at least I had conceived a child with you before your flight, if only
some little Aeneas were playing in my court who by his look could remind me of you, then I would not seem so utterly vanquished and abandoned.]

(*A.* 4.327–30)

Parvulus is called the only true diminutive in the *Aeneid,* and commentators connect this passage with the end of Catullus' first epithalamion
(61):[14]

---

12. "eine der zartesten Stellen des Gedichts"; for meter and language see Norden 1957,
429 n. 1; cf. Wlosok 1967, 139–42.

13. E.g., 62.39–42, 64.87–90; see chapter 2. *Amaracus* is a rare word in Latin, appearing
before Vergil only once, in Catullus' first epithalamion (61.7).

14. See Pease 1935, *ad loc.,* for bibliography and comment.

Torquatus volo parvulus
matris e gremio suae
porrigens teneras manus
dulce rideat ad patrem
semihiante labello.

[Would that a baby Torquatus, stretching forth his little hands from his
mother's lap, laugh sweetly at his father with breathless lips.]

(61.216–20)

Parvulus Torquatus will increase a venerable family but will also guaran-
tee the *pudicitia* of Vinia by his likeness to his father:

sit suo similis patri
Manlio et facile insciis
noscitetur ab omnibus
et pudicitiam suae
matris indicet ore.

[Let him look like his father Manlius, and let him be known at once to
all who see him, and prove his mother's virtue by his face.]

(61.222–25)

The resemblance of son and father as proof of a mother's fidelity is a
conceit with primarily cultural associations. As far back as Hesiod it is
included among the canonical features of various utopian states: in the
just city, for example (*Works and Days* 225–47), so long as Peace roams the
earth, the land produces food spontaneously, men live without labor and
seafaring, and women "bring forth children like their parents,"
[τίκτουσιν δὲ γυναῖκες ἐοικότα τέκνα γονεῦσιν].[15] Here Vergil reverses
the conceit: Dido's *parvulus Aeneas* would prove the father's faithlessness,
and any likeness to Aeneas would remind her that she, having broken her
oath to Sychaeus, has been betrayed and abandoned. As it is she gets neither Aeneas nor any reminder of him:

agit ipse furentem
in somnis ferus Aeneas, semperque relinqui
sola sibi, semper longam incomitata videtur
ire viam et Tyrios deserta quaerere terra.

15. See West 1980, 213–21. Fordyce (1961, *ad loc.*) compares Horace *Odes* 4.5.23,
laudantur simili prole puerperae [girls are praised for their children who look like them],
and Martial 6.27.3.

[In her dreams cruel Aeneas drove her on as she raved, and always she seemed to be alone and abandoned, lonely in long wandering, seeking her people in deserted places.]

(*A.* 4.465–68)

At simul quae sit poteris cognoscere virtus . . .

According to the vocabulary of the poem, hunts and games distinguish boys from *iuvenes* and train them for warfare in the adult world. In Book 9 Numanus Remulus gives these conventional stages of growth:[16]

> venatu invigilant pueri silvasque fatigant,
> flectere ludus equos et spicula tendere cornu.
> at patiens operum parvoque adsueta iuventus
> aut rastris terram domat aut quatit oppida bello.

[Our boys spend days and nights at the hunt and in the woods; their play is to turn their horses through the course and to aim shafts with their bows. But our young men, inured to hard labor and grown accustomed to want, battle the earth with rakes or harry cities with war.]

(*A.* 9.605–8)

Two episodes, the *lusus Troiae* in Book 5 and the hunt in Book 7, illustrate the second stage of Iulus' development (Books 5–8).

The lusus Troiae

Much about the *lusus Troiae* is familiar from literature on Book 5 and need only be briefly summarized here. It is Vergil's fictional *aetion* for contemporary revivals of the game, first by Julius Caesar in 45 B.C. and then by Augustus. Its occurrence in the *Aeneid* asserts a continuity between past and present, both in the narrative time of the poem, *gaudentque tuentes . . . veterumque agnoscunt ora parentum* [they felt delight watching their sons . . . and recognized in them the faces of their forbears] (*A.* 5.575–76), and in the time of the Republic, *Troiaque nunc pueri, Troianum dicitur agmen* [and today the boys are called Troy, the band is called Trojan] (*A.* 5.602). Though the *lusus* ostensibly prepares boys for war,[17] in Vergil's poem and

---

16. Camilla spends her childhood hunting with *tela puerilia* [a child's weapons] (*A.* 11.576–80); Lausus is *equum domitor debellatorque ferarum* [breaker of horses and conqueror of wild beasts] (*A.* 7.651), which Conington (1963, *ad loc.*) calls his training for war. On hunts as preparations for adulthood and as initiatory rites see Lonis 1979, 200–203. For stages of a human lifetime, see chapter 1 and "*Saeclorum ordo*" in chapter 6.

17. On *ludi* as real military exercises see Taylor 1924.

in Augustan Rome its real value is as an emblem of heroic antiquity to hold up to the children of the present, a device to spur them to the glories of the past.[18]

These are the main narrative and historical facts about the *lusus*. Interpretation is more problematical. Critics have addressed the boys' innocence and their distance from the gloom and death in the fourth book and from the preceding *certamina* of the fifth (strangely disturbing in their own way), and they have concluded that the game is "a concrete representation of optimism": at least in the new blood of old Troy there is promise of respite from wandering, loss, and pain, and some reason to hope for the future.[19]

Some scholars have revised this view and suggest that the imitation and anticipation of war in the game void any optimism it might have: *pugnaeque cient simulacra sub armis* [the boys formed into bands, a sham battle under arms] (*A.* 5.585).[20] Though the gist of these reassessments is correct, Vergil seems to say little about simple "warfare,"[21] and the details of the passage point elsewhere. What precisely does the *lusus* anticipate? In the night episode in Book 9 Euryalus sets out to become a hero; he instead creeps through the darkness killing enemies as they sleep, and the world he encounters repays his newfound *virtus* with death (see chapter 3). The issues in Book 9 are not about war and peace, as I have argued: the fall of Troy in *Aeneid* 2 provides the features of Vergil's night landscape and suggests that the threats of Laomedon's Troy have surfaced again, now in Italy, to entangle another generation and other nations. The imagery and vocabulary of the fall of Troy pervade the *lusus* as well, and with the same effect.

---

18. Heinze (1915, 157–79) gives most of these details and stresses the game's symbolic value; see more recently Holt 1980. The view that the *virtus* of the past can improve the present age is a republican and Augustan commonplace; see Augustus' own words, *Res Gestae* 8. On the revivals of the *lusus* to this end by Julius Caesar and by Augustus see Suetonius *Divi Augusti* 43, Last 1934, and Weinstock 1971, 88–90.

19. Feldman 1953, one of the few articles that attempts to discuss Iulus in any depth. See again the enthusiastic assessments of Heinze (1915, 157–59), Henry (1873–92, vol. 2, *ad A.* 5.545–602), and Hunt (1973, 75–77).

20. Putnam 1962, 221: "but even here [in the *lusus*] there remains in the background the potentiality of war when fought by men whose goal is death, not stage play"; cf. Baker 1985.

21. For arguments against Vergil's supposed "pacifism" see Lyne 1983 and Stahl 1981. I argue that the dangers in the narrative are historical and cultural; war is one symptom of the Trojan legacy, not the legacy itself.

Atys, Iulus, and Priam (the grandson of his namesake) lead groups of riders. Priam leads the first:

> una acies iuvenum, ducit quam parvus ovantem
> nomen avi referens Priamus, tua clara, Polite,
> progenies, auctura Italos.

[There was one troop of youths whom the child Priam, bearing his grandfather's name, led in their delight; he is your glorious offspring, Polites, destined to increase the Italian race.]

(A. 5.563–65)

Parvus Priamus and the mention of Polites conjure up the death of Priam on the last day of Troy: Neoptolemus stands in the doors of Priam's palace,

> qualis ubi in lucem coluber mala gramina pastus,
> frigida sub terra tumidum quem bruma tegebat,
> nunc, positis novus exuviis nitidusque iuventa,
> lubrica convolvit sublato pectore terga
> arduus ad solem, et linguis micat ore trisulcis.

[. . . just as a snake who comes forth into the light, battened on poisonous grasses, whom the winter covered, swollen under the frozen earth; now renewed with skin shed, and gleaming in youthful strength, it rolls its oily back with its chest raised high to the sun; the forked tongue flashes from its mouth.]

(A. 2.471–75)

The simile is (in part) from the final meeting of Hector and Achilles (*Il.* 22.93–95),[22] a prelude to a duel between heroes of more or less equal stature. The *impares vires* motif that characterizes Troy and the epic world elsewhere in the *Aeneid* (the killing of "children" by adult warriors)[23] appears here in reverse, the old man killed by the young, the son of Achilles killing the father of Hector. Priam embodies not only Troy itself[24] but also the older age of heroes that dies along with him, and Priam's taunts to Neoptolemus mark this change in the world: *at non ille, satum quo te mentiris, Achilles / talis in hoste fuit Priamo* [You, liar, are not the son of that

---

22. Conington 1963 and Austin 1964, both *ad loc.*

23. E.g., Achilles and Troilus (*A.* 1.474); Turnus and Pallas: *prior Pallas, si qua fors adiuvet ausum / viribus imparibus* (*A.* 10.459); and Aeneas and Lausus, *quo moriture ruis maioraque viribus audes* (*A.* 11.811). See Knauer 1964, 304–8, for discussion.

24. See Heinze 1915, 42–44.

Achilles, who was never as you are to Priam, his enemy] (*A.* 2.540–41).[25]
Vergil's old men believe in heroism and try to invest the young with their
belief, as Evander tries with Pallas (see chapter 4), and as old Aletes, *annis
gravis*, tries with Nisus and Euryalus (*A.* 9.246–56). In the *Aeneid* the old
world and heroism are dead, and this belief and this attempted investi-
ture are futile.

The boys ride *ante ora parentum* [before their parents' eyes] (*A.* 5.553), a
heroic *topos* to which we should compare Aeneas' first words in the poem,
beati . . . ora patrum Troiae sub moenibus altis [Happy are those who died beneath the high walls of Troy, before the eyes of their fathers] (*A.* 1.95), as
well as the words of Aeneas' "model," Odysseus, lost at sea (*Od.* 5.306–11):
to die nobly in battle before one's people or family (if one must die) is the
aim and the reward of all good heroes.[26] Vergil adapts this conventional
beatitude to the new world of failure and loss, and outside of the *lusus* it
is always a formula for deaths and funerals, typically of children.[27] The
phrase occurs most memorably, of course, in the death of Polites, *ante ora
patris* (*A.* 2.663), and *ante oculis . . . et ora parentum* (*A.* 2.531); still a third
time we find the sense, if not the same words, in Priam's reproach to
Neoptolemus: *qui nati coram me cernere letum / fecisti et patrios foedasti funere
vultus* [You, Neoptolemus, who made me watch the death of my son and
polluted a father's eyes with death] (*A.* 2.538–39).

We can note, finally, that Ascanius leads his *agmen* on a horse given to
him by Dido (*A.* 5.571–72). Allusions to Dido or her gifts have figured in
the story of Nisus and Euryalus and in that of Pallas,[28] and here we are
again reminded that her betrayal and death characterize the epic world
and not the valor or the heroism that the *lusus* leads us to anticipate.
Polites and Priam, Dido, and the deaths of children refute the heroic
ethos that the *lusus* represents; Ascanius will inherit, implicitly, a different reality, a reality that these characters and these deaths define.

The suggestion of these details, the intimations of a different reality
behind the heroic window dressing of Book 5, culminate, as by now we
might expect, with an allusion to Catullus. Vergil describes the turnings
of the horses as the windings of a labyrinth:

---

25. Cf. Dido's reproaches to Aeneas, *A.* 4.365–67, and Knauer 1964, 387, for Homeric
parallels.

26. Stahl (1981) has a good discussion of these lines.

27. The words are used at *G.* 4.447 (= *A.* 6.308) to describe the *pueri innuptaeque puellae,
/ impositique rogis iuvenes* [boys and unmarried girls, and young men placed on their
funeral pyres] in the underworld; this repetition is noted by Putnam (1965): "the phrase
recalls more sorrow than joy" (220).

28. See chapters 3 and 4.

ut quondam Creta fertur Labyrinthus in alta
parietibus textum caecis iter ancipitemque
mille viis habuisse dolum, qua signa sequendi
frangeret indeprensus et inremeabilis error.

[Thus long ago, they say, a labyrinth in lofty Crete had a course that
wound through blind walls and had an insoluble puzzle with countless
paths, where the baffling and untrackable maze broke any hope of re-
tracing.]

(*A.* 5.588–91)

Although the comparison of the *lusus* to a labyrinth occurs first in the
sixth century and seems to be traditional,[29] Vergil's simile clearly suggests Catullus. Catullan themes have figured in all the *pueri* discussed
thus far, and this allusion conforms to type. The labyrinth is Catullus'
denunciation of the heroic world, yet another image by which that
world's anachronistic ideals are shown to be false. Theseus' motives are
those of a traditional hero:

ipse suum Theseus pro caris corpus Athenis
proicere optavit potius quam talia Cretam
funera Cecropiae nec funera portarentur.

[Theseus hoped to give his own life for Athens' sake rather than let his
people be brought, like living dead, to Crete.]

(64.81–83)

He seeks a hero's rewards, *aut mortem . . . aut praemia laudis* [either death
or the rewards of glory] (64.102), by conventional inspiration, *fervida virtus* (64.218). His labor is not the conventional duel with a monster (Heracles and Cacus, for example) but an *error*, a *dolus*, which he must unravel.
Catullus subordinates his victory over the Minotaur to the subsequent
betrayals by and of Ariadne and to Aegeus' death. *Virtus* is inimical to
familial love and the domestic world, tearing Theseus from his father, *tua
fervida virtus / eripit invito mihi te* [your burning virtue tore you away from

29. Putnam 1962, 220. The *lusus* and the labyrinth are commonly connected, first on a
sixth-century vase that shows equestrians, a maze pattern, and the word *truia* (*Troia?*); see
Taylor 1924, 160–61, and, for description and interpretation, Knight 1967, 202–14. Pliny,
too, (*N. H.* 36.85) compares the real labyrinths he has seen and studied with stones in the
Campus Martius that marked the route of the horses in *ludi: quae itinerum ambages
occursusque ac recursus inexplicabilis continet;* Pliny's description (*ambages, inexplicabilis*)
seems to depend on Vergil's, as most seem to after the time of the *Aeneid;* cf. Pomponius
Mela *de Chorographia* 1.56. But Varro's *inextricabilis* (cited by Pliny at *N. H.* 36.91) predates
the *Aeneid.*

me, against my wishes] (64.218–19), and causing his father's suicide.[30]
Love draws Ariadne from the security and innocence of childhood and
from her mother's embrace:

> hunc simul ac cupido conspexit lumine virgo
> regia, quam suavis exspirans castus odores
> lectulus in molli complexu matris alebat,
> quales Eurotae praecingunt flumina myrtus
> aurave distinctos educit verna colores,
> non prius ex illo flagrantia declinavit
> lumina, quam cuncto concepit corpore flammam.

[Once the royal maiden, Ariadne, gazed upon him with desire—she
whom the chaste bed, sweetly fragrant, still nurtured in her mother's
soft embrace, the bed as fragrant as the myrtles that line Eurota's
streams, or as the spring breeze when it brings forth a flood of color—
she did not avert her burning gaze from him before her whole body
blazed with fire.]

(64.86–92)

The lines that begin and end the passage, Ariadne inflamed with love for
Theseus, are a world away from the images of nurture and softness they
frame, the pain of adulthood against the innocence of the child, the fire
of love against pastoral shade.[31] Catullus locates all sensations of color,
touch, and especially smell in the symbol of Ariadne's metamorphosis
from child and daughter, to lover: *castus lectulus*, the chaste bed. These
oppositions recall those of the epithalamia and of poem 65 (see chapter
2), a childhood of secure embraces and fragrant retreats, and the desola-
tions of adult love. If we strip away the heroic machinery and the celebrated names and the places of poem 64, we find the constant themes of
Catullus' verse—*immemor, desertus, letum*—which are nothing more than
Catullus' vision of adult reality.

The labyrinth, Dido, Polites, and Priam define the reality that awaits
the boys when they become adults, and they reveal as illusions martial
glory and continuity with the heroic past. The *lusus* concludes with a
final contrast between a heroic fantasy and epic reality. When Juno tricks

---

30. Catullus consistently represents *virtus* as destructive. Compare the *virtus* of Achilles
in the same poem (*illius egregias virtutes claraque facta / saepe fatebuntur gnatorum in funere
matres*, 64.348–49) and similarly 64.51, 323, 357. The only other instance of the word in
Catullus occurs at 68.90, which describes the "death" of virtue at Troy: *Troia virum et
virtutum omnium acerba cinis*; see Ross 1975, 13–14.

31. On Catullus' use of "framing" lines see 8.1–8 and Fraenkel 1961, 51–53; on the
dominance of fire over shade in Vergil see "The Hunt" and n. 34 in this chapter.

the Trojan women into burning the ships, Ascanius rushes forward to stop them:

> 'quis furor iste novus? quo nunc, quo tenditis,' inquit,
> 'heu miserae cives? non hostem inimicaque castra
> Argivum, vestras spes uritis. en, ego vester
> Ascanius!'—galeam ante pedes proiecit inanem,
> qua ludo indutus belli simulacra ciebat.

["What new madness is this? Where do you expect to go now, wretched women, my fellow citizens? You are not burning the camps of the Argive enemy but your own hopes. Look, it is I, your Ascanius!" With that he threw at their feet his useless helmet, which he had worn for playing at the mock battles.]

(A. 5.670–74)

Non hostem inimicaque castra / Argivum is not the obvious thing to say, now seven years after the fall of Troy; burning ships, with Iulus' reminder of Troy and the Argive camps, must suggest the *aristeia* of Troy's greatest hero, the burning of the ships by Hector in *Iliad* 15–16. In the *Aeneid* Homeric heroes and *kleos* have been displaced; we find instead women and children and the constant realities of Vergil's poem: treachery, and *furor* born from deception, grief, and long suffering. The *belli simulacra* as a celebration of heroic valor and its flowering in youth are, in this world, useless—thus *inanem* (673), the epithet of Ascanius' helmet[32]—against the realities that in this scene and in the future will confront Ascanius, just as they have his father. The labyrinth is neither a descriptive ornament nor so narrowly a figure for the wars destined to come, *fato bella ventura*

---

32. Vergil repeats *galeam inanem* from his lament for the civil wars at the end of the first *Georgic:* at some future time in a pacified world farmers will uncover the ancient remains of their ancestors (the men of Vergil's generation): *gravibus rastris galeas pulsabit inanis / grandiaque effossis mirabitur ossa sepulcris* [he will strike the hollow helmets with heavy rakes and marvel at the giant bones dug out from graves] (G. 1.496–97). *Inanis,* "hollow," suggests the sound made by striking, as Conington (1963, *ad loc.*) notes, but it implies also "useless," the folly of human vanities: even the men of old, greater than the men of today, return to dust, their arms rusted and their passions and blood spent for nothing.

Inanem at A. 5.673 has caused much needless trouble. Servius (*ad loc.: concavam, vacuam, sine capite* [hollow, empty, without a head in it]) is followed reluctantly by Conington (1963, *ad loc.*), Williams (1960, *ad loc.*), and others. Henry's objections (1873–92, vol. 2, *ad loc.*) to this and other interpretations are correct; his own solution, though it gives the word its proper meaning, "useless," does not go far enough: "the moment Ascanius left the battle the helmet . . . became a *galea inanis,* a mere helmet and nothing more." Vergil's epithet is surprising and significant and can only be understood in the terms of the whole passage.

(see "*Spes gentis,*" in this chapter); rather it identifies the *lusus Troiae* as a preface to the losses we find everywhere in the world of the poem.

The Hunt

The hunt in Latium and the killing of the tame stag is the second training passage of Iulus' middle stage. Iulus responds like a young hero, *ipse etiam eximiae laudis succensus amore / Ascanius*, the words used of Euryalus' heroic impulse, *obstipuit amore / Euryalus* (*A.* 9.197–98). Iulus is "inflamed," *succensus,* and the metaphor, though perhaps long dead,[33] is revived and given point by the surrounding imagery and language. The stag belongs to cool and shade: *fluvio cum forte secundo / deflueret ripaque aestus viridante levaret* [He chanced to be floating down with the current, escaping the heat by the lush riverbanks] (*A.* 7.494–95). Iulus' heroic (or preheroic) deed is transformed and emerges in the poem as a fire that invades and destroys the coolness of the pastoral shade. Allecto, an image of destructive fire in the preceding passage (*A.* 7.445–66), causes Iulus' hounds to burn (*ardentes,* *A.* 7.481), and the death of the stag enkindles the countryside, *belloque animos accendit agrestis* [it incited rustic hearts to war] (*A.* 7.482).

These metaphors are conventional and Vergil's touch is light. Of chief interest here are the comparisons with the deception of Dido in Book 1 (and the comparable use of fire and shade) and with the hunt in Book 4. Iulus is not involved in the deception of Dido; he is physically removed from the action of the scene. In the hunt in Book 7 he is agent, himself a burning force invading the pastoral *umbra.*[34] The "marriage" of Aeneas and Dido is the main event of the hunt in Book 4, *primaque malorum / causa fuit* [this was the beginning of many evils] (*A.* 4.169–70), while Iulus' role is minor, as it is throughout the first quarter of the poem. Vergil's near repetition of the phrase in Book 7 connects the passages, but here Iulus is in the foreground, responsible, if not culpable, for the beginning of *labor* in Italy: *prima laborum / causa fuit* (*A.* 7.481–82).[35]

---

33. See Norden 1957, *ad A.* 6.5 (*emicat ardens*).

34. Compare the same epic and pastoral effects in Catullus 64 (see "The *luses Troiae*" in chapter 5) and in *Aeneid* 8: Venus brings Aeneas the arms of Vulcan in a remote valley by cool water (*egelido secretum flumine, A.* 8.610). Here, as always, epic heat overwhelms pastoral shade: the arms glow blood red (*sanguineam, A.* 8.622) and gleam with flame—*qualis cum caerula nubes / solis inardescit radiis longeque refulget* [as when cerulean cloud turns to flame in the rays of the sun and sends back its fire far and wide] (*A.* 8.622–23).

35. Scheinberg (1982) discusses the particular connection of this word with the Trojans.

THE INITIATION OF IULUS

Aeneas' journey up the Tiber to Pallanteum is a metaphorical return to youth and to heroic innocence, both parts of a kind of primitivism.[36] The parallels between Aeneas and Telemachus, the suggestion of Telemachus' youth and inexperience in the figure of Evander, and the anachronistic heroism of Evander and Pallas (and Evander's Heracles), mark Pallanteum as a cultural oasis. Youth, heroism, and primitivism are equated, and all belong outside the world of Vergil's poem.

As Aeneas figuratively moves back in time to the world's "childhood," Ascanius moves in the opposite direction, to a reenactment of the siege and fall of Troy, which for the *Aeneid* is the inevitable culmination of civilization and the definitive revelation of the falseness of the heroic ethos. Iulus is left in charge of the camp (called *Troia, A.* 10.378) and is responsible for duties beyond his years: *ante annos animumque gerens curamque virilem (A.* 9.311). He imitates the words and gestures of adulthood, recalling, in his role as head of the assembly, Agamemnon or Nestor, and he presides over a repetition of the *Doloneia,* the Iliadic archetype of deception. Iulus inherits his father's world, not just warfare and *labor,* but Troy itself.

The initiation of Pallas at Aeneas' side as they travel by night toward the Trojan camp (*A.* 10.158–61) is less dramatic than Iulus' first act of war, but the elements are the same. Pallas' first navigation by stars (*opacae / noctis iter, A.* 10.161–62) and his exposure to Aeneas' deeds (*quae passus terraque marique, A.* 10.162) suggest delicately but clearly that the boy is leaving behind his youth and its illusions.

Iulus' initiation to the adult world is abrupt and explicit. The child and hunter of the seventh book becomes a warrior in Book 9 with his first killing of a man:

> tum primum bello celerem intendisse sagittam
> dicitur ante feras solitus terrere fugacis
> Ascanius, fortemque manu fudisse Numanum.

[Then for the first time Ascanius is said to have aimed a swift arrow in battle, until now accustomed to routing beasts in flight, and he brought down strong Numanus with his own hand.]

(*A.* 9.590–92)

---

36. See "The Heroic Education of Pallas" in chapter 4.

Tum primum connects Iulus with the poem's other boys on their first day of battle, and the change of targets, from *feras* (wild beasts) to *fortem . . . Numanum* is the beginning of manhood: boys hunt, in Numanus Remulus' program of growth, *venatu invigilant pueri,* and men wage war, *quatit oppida bello* (*A.* 9.605–8). Iulus perceives his shot as a beginning (*Iuppiter omnipotens, audacibus adnue coeptis, A.* 9.625), like Pallas in his prayer to Heracles as he faces Turnus (*coeptis ingentibus adsis, A.* 10.461). For this explicitly adult deed Ascanius earns his patronymic *Aenide* (*A.* 9.653), used only here in the poem, marking, with all the details in the passage, the end of his childhood.

His shot answers Remulus' mockery of Trojan *virtus:* boys in Latium learn to hunt, endure hardships, and then wage war as men; the Trojans love music, dance, and (their cardinal vice) finery:

> vobis picta croco et fulgenti murice vestis
> desidiae cordi, iuvat indulgere choreis,
> et tunicae manicas et habent redimicula mitrae.
> o vere Phrygiae, neque enim Phryges, ite per alta
> Dindyma, ubi adsuetis biforem dat tibia cantum.

> [A colored robe in saffron and shining purple is what you love best, and to indulge in dancing is your pleasure; your tunics have flowing sleeves and your turbans are ribboned. In truth, you are Phrygian women, not Phrygian men—go off to high Dindyma, where the flute plays its double-piped song.]

> (*A.* 9.614–18)

It would be a mistake to ignore the prominence Vergil gives these charges in such an important scene: Trojan "effeminacy" is a commonplace that Vergil refers to elsewhere (we need not call it his prevailing view),[37] and measuring the full weight of Iulus' act depends on our granting it some credence. Vergil plainly invites us to see the killing of Remulus not only as a stage in Iulus' personal evolution but, just as much, as a stage in Roman cultural evolution, a suggestion that in Iulus the *vitia* of the Trojan past are dead and that the fulfillment of the Augustan promise lies ahead.[38] The scenes that follow cast doubt on this suggestion, and Iulus'

---

37. Cf. Chloreus, *sacer Cybelo,* whose flowing robes and golden armor lure Camilla to her death (*A.* 11.768–93). On this and other aspects of Remulus' speech see Thomas 1982b, 145–60.

38. Similarities between Iulus and the *puer* of the fourth *Eclogue* are relevant here; see "*Spes gentis,*" in this chapter.

initiation becomes a version (though one that is more ambiguous) of the failed hopes we find throughout the poem.

Spes gentis

For Iulus' character this is a critical moment, yet Vergil stops. Apollo pulls Iulus back from his initiation (*cetera parce, puer, bello, A.* 9.656), and the reason can only be thematic. Iulus is the *spes gentis* who by the claims of the prophetic tradition will escape the past and the paradigms of his *gens*, reach the stars and give birth to gods:

> macte nova virtute, puer, sic itur ad astra,
> dis genite et geniture deos. iure omnia bella
> gente sub Assaraci fato ventura resident,
> nec te Troia capit.

[Boy, proud in your new manhood, thus men reach the stars, child born from gods and destined to give birth to gods. All wars fated to come under Assaracus' line will justly end, and Troy no longer holds you.]
(*A.* 9.641–44)

Apollo's declaration is plain enough and ought to permit no doubt: *nec te Troia capit*. The collocation *virtute puer* (an etymological schema)[39] suggests that Iulus will have both his new adulthood (*vir* in *virtute*) and the innocence of childhood (*puer*)—heroism with no taint of the past. Servius Danielis connects him in the act of killing Remulus to the boy of the fourth *Eclogue*,[40] and in expectation and in promise the comparison is apt. The long tyranny of history will end with Ascanius (as with the *puer* of the *Eclogue*), and the *priscae vestigia fraudis* [traces of ancient deception]

39. Vergil uses this etymology again in Aeneas' final speech to Iulus (see "Facta heroum," in this chapter). For the etymology *vir* in *virtute* see Cicero *Tusc.* 2.18.43 and Varro *L. L.* 5.73; Vergil's is less wooden than the usual device, e.g., Plautus *Amph.* 212, *viri freti virtute et viribus*, and Livy 21.4.9, *has tantas viri virtutes*.

40. The notice suggests an ancient interpretation rather than a casual observation: *ad A.* 9.621 Servius Danielis supplements Servius' explanation of Iulus' prayer to Jupiter: *quia omne initium <et incrementum> Iovi debetur* [because every beginning <and every stage of growth> is owed to Jupiter]. Danielis' addition of "incrementum" seems strange until we see that he is reading this passage side by side with *Ecl.* 4.49, *Iovis incrementum*; there he remarks, *nam in VIIII Ascanius in Numanum intendens sagittam, Iovem magis invocavit Iuppiter omnipotens* [In *Aeneid* 9 Ascanius, aiming an arrow at Numanus, invokes Jupiter, "Jupiter the all-powerful"]. Servius anticipates Wili (1930, 104–5), who equates Iulus and the boy of *Ecl.* 4 as "Weltherrscherkinder"; cf. Heinze 1915, 157 and 159, for similar (but more general) remarks about childhood. In chapter 6 I will treat more fully the connection between the themes of the *Aeneid* and the fourth *Eclogue*.

(*Ecl.* 4.31) and the *Laomedonteae . . . periuria Troiae* [perjuries of Laomedon's Troy] (*G.* 1.502), deplored so often and so clearly in Vergil's works, will at last lose their power to harm.

But what about the rest of Apollo's promise? *Resident* cannot mean that wars will not come, only that they will (someday) end; *bella,* furthermore, will surely come, by the command of fate, *fato ventura.* Most important, Vergil leaves the essential words in the prophecy ambiguous: Apollo either says that under Assaracus' descendants, *gente sub Assaraci,* the wars will end (*resident*), or, following word order more closely, that under Assaracus' line wars will come, as decreed by fate (*omnia bella / gente sub Assaraci fato ventura*); the wars will end, but the time and agent of peace are left unspecified.[41] The *labores,* the strengths, and the failures of Aeneas have implications for Augustus; so we naturally expect Iulus to reflect the ideals of the Augustan program and to suggest that the promise of the new regime will be realized. Vergil stops short of resolving the contradiction between this prophecy (the positive reading, at least) and the momentum of history: Iulus remains a child, stalled before his final emergence as either a miraculous agent of change (like the *puer* of the fourth *Eclogue*) or as an epic character who will carry ancestral "guilt" to later generations. The profession of deliverance remains only a promise, a formulaic hope for an always receding future.

Vergil does not fully write Iulus into history, and so the child remains indeterminate, an unsettling role for the pivotal character between Troy and Rome. Iulus' appearance in Book 10, however, puts his escape from the Trojan past in further doubt. Vergil interrupts the heroic catalog of Trojans on the battlements of the camp (*A.* 10.118–45) with a description of Iulus:

> ipse inter medios, Veneris iustissima cura,
> Dardanius caput, ecce, puer detectus honestum,
> qualis gemma micat fulvum quae dividit aurum,
> aut collo decus aut capiti, vel quale per artem
> inclusum buxo aut Oricia terebintho
> lucet ebur; fusos cervix cui lactea crinis
> accipit et molli subnectens circulus auro.

> [There in the middle stood the Dardanian boy himself, bareheaded, truest care of Venus, like a flashing gem that divides bright gold, finery for the neck or brow, or again, as ivory gleams when set in boxwood or Ori-

---

41. Fitzgerald translates Apollo's words to Iulus, "all fated wars / will quiet down, and justly, in the end / under descendants of Assaracus." On the ambiguities in Vergil's prophecies, particularly of Rome, see O'Hara 1990, especially 128–75.

cian terebinth; upon his milky neck his hair streamed, bound in pliant gold.]

(A. 10.132–38)

The language and the structure of this passage, as well as Iulus' inactivity, separate him from those fighting around him:[42] fourteen lines precede Iulus' description of seven lines, and seven lines follow. For some critics the simile is a praise of youth and beauty;[43] for others Iulus is lifeless and useless, with no hint of the heroic promise of Apollo's prophecy.[44] Vergil's passage has a parallel, however, that removes the question from the realm of impression and opinion and suggests that Iulus carries with him, despite Apollo's words, the seeds of Troy and the decline and decay that Troy has come to represent. *Aut Oricia terebintho* occurs at Propertius 3.7.49, where the Greek vocabulary and prosody support the sense of oriental finery and decadence.[45] Propertius connects Paetus' death at sea with cultural decline: the boy rejects the simple, rustic life that Propertius prescribes, *quod si contentus patrio bove verteret agros* [if only he had been content to plow his own fields with the family ox] (line 43; cf. *pauper,* line 46), and chooses the love of money and travel in the fallen world (lines 1–6). Seafaring traditionally marks the end of cultural innocence, and here the motif is elaborated, including both the extremes of violence and hardship for sailors (cf. lines 7–12), and the most decadent luxuries for passengers:

> non tulit hic Paetus stridorem audire procellae
> et duro teneras laedere fune manus
> sed thyio thalamo aut Oricia terebintho
> ecfultum pluma versicolore caput.

[Nor was Paetus the sort to endure the howling storms or to scrape his soft hands on the harsh ropes, but in a luxurious stateroom[46] paneled with cedar or with Orician terebinth, he rests his head on multicolored pillows of down.]

(3.7.47–50)

Propertius *Liber III* (25–20 B.C.)[47] and the *Aeneid* (ca. 26–19 B.C.) are

---

42. The other Trojan warriors have Homeric names and attributes—e.g., *fert ingens toto conixus corpore saxum, / haud partem exiguam montis, Lyrnesius Acmon* (127–28); see Conington 1963, *ad loc.*

43. Hornsby 1970, 116.

44. E.g., Block 1980, 137.

45. Smyth 1951, 75–77, especially: "in [line] 49 Propertius is almost speaking Greek" (76).

46. According to Smythe 1951, 76, *thalamo* refers to a stateroom or cabin.

47. On the dating of Propertius Book 3 see, conveniently, Camps 1966, 1.

roughly contemporary; there is no clear reason for either poet to quote so exactly from the other (note even the same hiatus before *aut*). Most likely both poems reproduce an earlier source (now lost) that described excess and opulence memorably enough to inspire these imitations,[48] Propertius' in a medley of stock motifs and predictable sentiments, Vergil's in a less obvious context. Vergil's simile associates Iulus, in his distance from the fighters around him, to the Trojan *luxuria* in Remulus' attack,[49] and Iulus' enforced childhood (*parce, puer, bello*), forestalls, but may not prevent, the consequences of his ancestry.

Facta heroum

Before his duel with Turnus Aeneas speaks his only words to Iulus in the poem:[50]

> disce, puer, virtutem ex me verumque laborem,
> fortunam ex aliis. nunc te mea dextera bello
> defensum dabit et magna inter praemia ducet.
> tu facito, mox cum matura adoleverit aetas,
> sis memor et te animo repetentem exempla tuorum
> et pater Aeneas et avunculus excitet Hector.

[From me, boy, learn what manhood means, and true hardship; learn good fortune from others. Now my right hand will defend you in battle and teach you the rewards of warfare. Be sure, when you become a man, to remember this, keeping in your heart the models you have from your people, and let your father Aeneas and your uncle Hector rouse you to greatness.]

(*A.* 12.435–40)

Aeneas' life is characterized by the first words of his speech, *virtus* and *labor*. *Virtus* means not only courage in war (Vergil's use of the word is conventional, unlike Catullus') but also adulthood by its etymological schema, *puer virtutem* (cf. *A.* 9.641); as such it becomes nearly a synonym for *labor*, the constant burden of humankind that recurs in the *Georgics*

---

48. For the difficulties with these lines and for possible solutions see Shackelton Bailey 1956, 150–51.

49. See "The Initiation of Iulus" in this chapter and Thomas 1982b, 146–60.

50. The main texts for comparison are Hector's speech to Astyanax (*Il.* 6.476–81) and Ajax' to his son, both in Sophocles *Ajax* 550 and in Accius *Iudicium Armorum* (frag. 123W): *virtuti sis par, dispar fortunis patris* [may you be your father's equal in virtue, but unlike him in fortune].

and in the underworld with *Letum, Discordia,* and *Metus* (*A.* 6.274–81). The adult world of *labor* is Iulus' legacy from Aeneas; father and uncle will indeed be his *exempla* when he enters manhood (*cum matura adoleverit aetas*), and their *labores* will be his own, unless he can escape his past. Our belief in his escape depends on prophecies that the world's real constraints, *virtus* (adulthood) and *labor,* and not simply their literary or "historical" expressions (*Troia, Laomedontis periuria,* and the rest), will someday by some heroic agency be overcome.

Though much in the poem argues against the belief in this agency, Vergil makes a theme of the belief itself and its persistence: we think again of Hector in *Iliad* 6, who knows that he is doomed and addresses his doomed son with the same illusions of hope in a heroic future.[51] Adults in the *Aeneid* try consistently to instill the young with their dreams of past greatness: Evander, with Pallas, and Nisus, with Euryalus, invest in this dream, and the *lusus Troiae* is a reflection of the same desire among Vergil's contemporaries.[52] The hope invested in youth and in the possibility of renewal and change—the belief that the world can be improved—makes the *lusus Troiae* more than a game or "training"; in the poem it implies a remedy or at least recompense for Troy, Creusa, Anchises, and Dido, as it does in Vergil's time for the failing stock of Roman *virtus.* The hope of a final victory over past and present realities is the heart of Augustan policy and propaganda, and it is no surprise that Vergil makes so much of it in the *Aeneid.* Heinze summarizes this climate of hope in Vergil's day:

> [Augustus] yearned so passionately to see a new generation spring up from the blood-sodden battlefields of the civil wars, a generation which, innocent of the guilt of their fathers, would be able to reap the fruits of decades of slaughter.[53]

This belief is the focus of the rest of Aeneas' speech. Contrary to the experience of his own life and his domination by struggle and loss, Aeneas clings to a fantasy of heroism for his son: the father's "iron age" struggles will make the world safe and the child secure (*nunc te mea dextera bello / defensum dabit*) and will provide Iulus with a world in which conventional heroism is valued again (*magna inter praemia ducet*). Aeneas must do the dirty work of empire building; he cannot even remove his helmet to kiss

---

51. Cf. especially *Il.* 6.447–49.
52. See "The *lusus Troiae*" in this chapter.
53. Heinze 1915, 159 (= 1993, 129); cf. especially Norden 1966, 373–75 (= 1901, 263–64), and Syme 1939, 217–20.

his son (*summaque per galeam delibans oscula fatur, A.* 12.434), and there is no respite from the epic world, no return to the role of father (the brief consolation granted to Hector in the *Iliad*).[54] The father must suffer, work, and lose nearly everything he loves (wife, father, lover); the future and lasting peace belong to Iulus.[55]

The civil wars produced a generation apparently still burdened by their fathers' guilt, and Augustus' hope for a rich posterity went unmet. The heirs of the ruined Republic seemed unable to "reap the fruits" of their predecessors' struggles, in light of Augustus' failed attempts to produce a successor and to rebuild the Roman patriciate: Rome, *felix prole virum*, remained only a dream.[56] The *Aeneid* itself repeatedly suggests that these hopes are illusory, as Aeneas' final words to Iulus convey: *et animo repetentem exempla tuorum / et pater Aeneas et avunculus excitet Hector* (*A.* 12.439–40). Aeneas repeats the words of Andromache, the character in the poem most tragically lost in the fantasies of the past (*A.* 12.440 = *A.* 3.342). Though married twice since the fall of Troy and with a son by Neoptolemus, she remains *coniunx Hectorea* (*A.* 3.488), haunting an empty tomb of her dead husband in a miniature Troy. Her concern for Ascanius is that he remember his lost mother (he is Andromache's Astyanax in a world of surrogates) and that he be stirred to *antiquam virtutem* (*A.* 3.341–42) by his father and the memory of *avunculus Hector*. The present and reality mean nothing to Andromache and we expect her illusions of the heroic past to remain. It is more striking that these illusions emerge at the end of the poem in Aeneas. The persistence of illusion from one generation to the next (despite all evidence) is one of the poem's most profound ironies and one of Vergil's most important observations. In the *Aeneid* human life consists of childhood illusions (heroism and valor), followed by the *labor* and pain of adulthood and, in later life, the false dream that final salvation can be won, though won mainly for others.

Marcellus and Romana potens

Apollo's prophecy and Aeneas' final words to Iulus should be considered in the light of another prophecy and another *puer*, Marcellus.[57] Late in the

---

54. See Edwards 1960 and Schadewaldt 1965, 215–17.
55. Cf. Venus' speech at *A.* 10.45–53.
56. See Anchises' praise of the Roman future in Book 6 with Norden's comment quoted in "Vergil and the Coming of Age" in chapter 1.
57. With this section see especially Feeney 1986 and O'Hara 1990.

poem Juno's hatred for the Trojans softens and she yields at last to the will of Jupiter and fate:

> sit Latium, sint Albani per saecula reges,
> sit Romana potens Itala virtute propago:
> occidit, occideritque sinas cum nomine Troia.

[Let Latium remain, let the Alban kings remain through the ages, let Roman generations grow strong in Italian manhood. But Troy is dead, and let Troy, with her name, lie dead.]

(*A.* 12.826–28)

Only the duel between Turnus and Aeneas remains, a final obstacle before the *imperium sine fine* can begin. This forecast, it seems, can only be hopeful: Troy must fade, but the new Roman stock will flourish, without, perhaps, the legacy of Troy, *occiderit . . . cum nomine Troia.*[58]

In Book 6 Aeneas' look into the future of his *gens* concludes with Anchises' epitaph for Marcellus; his words are echoed by and gloss Juno's prophecy and serve as a historical corrective to a mythical promise:

> o gnate, ingentem luctum ne quaere tuorum;
> ostendent terris hunc tantum fata nec ultra
> esse sinent. nimium vobis Romana propago
> visa potens, superi, propria haec si dona fuissent.

[My son, don't seek to know your people's greatest grief; fate will only show this man to the earth for a moment and then allow him to live no more. The stock of Rome would have seemed to you too powerful, gods above, if gifts so great had remained among us.]

(*A.* 6.868–71)

Propago (870) for "*gens*" or "race" is a notable archaism and rare in poetry before Vergil.[59] It occurs in the *Aeneid* only at these two passages,[60] and, with the repetition of *Romana* and *potens,* connects the two scenes.

Marcellus contradicts the prophetic optimism of the poem, the flowering of the *Hectorea gens*[61] through Iulus. The reality of Pallas, Euryalus,

58. Feeney (1991, 144–49) has an impressive discussion of this passage.

59. Lucretius uses it (1.42, 5.1027; cf. 4.998) in contexts that are probably Ennian; see Norden 1957, *ad A.* 6.868 ff. (p. 344), and Ennius frag. 442–43 Skutsch for the hapax *propagmen: nobis unde forent fructus vitaeque propagmen.*

60. Vergil uses it twice (meaning "shoot") in the *Georgics,* at 2.23 and 2.63.

61. The phrase itself, part of Jupiter's prophecy of future Roman greatness (*A.* 1.273), can only be ironic in light of Andromache and Astyanax; cf. Norden 1957, *ad A.* 6.781, quoted under "Vergil and the Coming of Age" in chapter 1.

and Lausus does not end but continues to haunt the Roman race, and Juno's words do not come true by the end of the poem or by the end of Vergil's lifetime. The world that Vergil describes demands the life or the soul of children before they can arrive at adulthood. What can Vergil do with Iulus? The failures of Vergil's own day are reflected in the world of the *Aeneid,* and in both worlds deliverance hangs uneasily between the facts of the past and present, and the promises of the future. Professions of ultimate redemption in the poem (via Iulus) are no different from those of Vergil's own time (via Marcellus), and neither can convince.

Vergil departs from the simple conventions of cultural pathology (ancient excellence and degenerate modernity). The deaths of children, and the failure of heroism and of prophecies of redemption are not the circumstantial tragedies of a grand cultural evolution that the *Aeneid* is intended to record and serve. As the *Eclogues* argue the tyranny of *amor* and the failure of literary *medicinae,* and as the *Georgics* describe the failure of *veterum praecepta* and the unrelenting domination by *labor,* these losses in the *Aeneid* refute claims that life can be fundamentally changed by politics, prophecy, or human effort.

CHAPTER VI

The Art of Escape and the Fourth Eclogue

Though Samuel Beckett may never before have been mentioned in the same breath with Vergil, his work reflects precisely the theme I would like to discuss in the fourth *Eclogue.* An untitled poem from *Poèmes* (1978) sketches a scene familiar from B movies and adolescent daydreams:

> I would like my love to die,
> and the rain to be falling on her grave
> and on me walking the streets
> mourning the first and last to love me.

The narrator longs to replace love with a more comfortable sensation—a manageable Hollywood grief, complete with set, lighting, and script; the poem invites increasing immersion in these reveries until one almost forgets the comic (perhaps) desperation of its premise, "I would like my love to die." Beckett's character, as his characters ritually do when faced with disorder and suffering, attempts a kind of storytelling, a headlong flight into the protection of narrative, in an effort to make emotion comprehensible and therefore endurable. Beckett explores the persistent fact of self-delusion and self-invention, for him the foundation art of living, the most human act.

The ancient lines of escape from chaos and fear are essentially the same as the modern. Beckett's character flees emotional chaos, while the concerns of Vergil's poetry are more global, including both the world of emotion and that of politics, but both poets observe the retreat into fantasy as a human constant. In the preceding chapters I have tried to account for a certain despair in the *Aeneid,* a despair much of the time answered only by vague premonitions and fervent optatives: *si qua fata aspera rumpas . . . ; tu Marcellus eris.*[1] What human ingenuity could

---

1. See "Marcellus and *Romana potens*" in chapter 5, and compare Anchises' plea to Pompey and Caesar, *ne pueri ne tanta animis adsuescite bella, / neu patriae validas in viscera vertite viris* [Do not, boys, learn the habit of wars so great, and do not turn your power against the vitals of your own nation] (*A.* 6.832–33). Fantasies of the future go hand in hand with rewritings of the past: Aeneas leaves the underworld by the gate of ivory (*A.* 6.893–901) as a *falsum insomnium,* whose human proportions and failings, Vergil implies, will be forgotten as the mythologies of later generations increasingly perfect him.

recompense, much less foresee or prevent, the death of Marcellus or the endemic loss of posterity for which his death is an emblem? Compensation is out of the question: belief in the future, however remote, is the sole refuge. The time in which the *Aeneid* was written (26–19 B.C.) was one of uncertain calm and perhaps tentative hope; Iulus is therefore an unfinished character, showing disturbing tendencies but also some possibility for change. The *Eclogues* chronicle an earlier and much worse period, anarchic times in which the need for deliverance became most desperate.[2] The fourth *Eclogue* (39 B.C.) was composed within five years of Caesar's assassination, only a few years after Philippi; the poem is usually read as Vergil's expression of relief at the cessation of these events, at the brief hope that their resolution offered. I instead suggest that Vergil, like Beckett, neither invests in nor endorses the fantasies he describes; like Beckett, he acts as self-conscious observer and recorder of the need for escape and of the imagery and vocabulary from which these fantasies are created.

ECLOGUE 4

Scholars have reconstructed a plausible sequence of events behind the composition of the fourth *Eclogue*: the Pact of Brundisium under Pollio's consulship in 40 B.C. and a child conceived in a politically significant marriage (though all identities are still debated) inspired in Vergil a vision of lasting peace for Rome. Vergil seems overwhelmed by optimism—an attitude rare in the *Eclogues,* but the new treaty and the anticipated birth gave hope. Although the pact between Octavian and Antony collapsed almost immediately, and though no *puer* was ever born, in 39 B.C. Vergil wrote his "prophecy" under these twin spells, and he included the poem when the collection was published four years later.[3]

---

2. Cf. Norden 1966, 400–421. Horace's *Epode* 16 responds to the same terrors and bitterly reproaches Rome for another decade of failure, *altera iam teritur bellis civilibus aetas / suis et ipsa Roma viribus ruit* [now another generation is worn down by civil war, and Rome is brought to ruin by her own hand] (1–2); Horace, like Vergil, proposes mock solutions for ills without remedy: abandon Italy for the Isles of the Blest; set sail for paradise—*secunda / ratem occupare quid moramur alite?* [why delay preparing a ship to sail when the omens are good?] (23–24).

3. Clausen (1982, 19–21) summarizes the most reasonable account of contemporary history, identifying the marriage as that of Antony and Octavia consummating Brundisium (40 B.C.), and their child as Vergil's *puer,* though a daughter was born rather than a son.

So far so good. But when one looks at the poem's details, consensus evaporates, except perhaps for the general agreement that there are problems too serious to ignore. To name only the two most obvious: the *ultima aetas* (by any known definition) should not be interrupted by the reemergence of the Iron Age, and the *ordo saeclorum* (if *saeculum* has any conventional meaning) should not evolve in a human lifetime. The poem seems to defy explication, and contemporary history, whether accurately reconstructed or not, provides no help. Vergil has purposely created enigmas, and I suggest that if we abandon our expectations and let these problems lead us, solutions will arise from the poem itself.

Saeclorum ordo

The center of the fourth *Eclogue* (lines 18–45) maps the progress simultaneously of a boy's life and (seemingly) of world ages: from the golden age during his infancy (8 lines) to transitional adolescence (5 lines), followed by an iron age (6 lines), and a second golden age in later life (11 lines).[4] Günther Jachmann correctly notes that all interpretations of the poem stand or fall on the reemergence of the iron age,[5] and I will begin there where the problems are most clear:

> pauca tamen suberunt priscae vestigia fraudis
> quae temptare Thetim ratibus, quae cingere muris
> oppida, quae iubeant telluri infindere sulcos.
> alter erit tum Tiphys, et altera quae vehat Argo
> delectos heroas; erunt etiam altera bella
> atque iterum ad Troiam magnus mittetur Achilles.

[Even so, a few traces of ancestral treachery will lie hidden, which bid us venture on the sea in ships, ring our cities with walls, dig furrows in the earth. Then there will be another Tiphys, and another Argo will carry picked heroes; there will even be wars again, and a second time great Achilles will be sent to Troy.]

(*Ecl.* 4.31–36)

Walled towns, agriculture, and warfare do not spring up and vanish from one decade to the next: Vergil's chronology is clearly impossible and has

---

4. Vergil follows the four standard Roman divisions of a human lifetime; see Ovid *Met.* 15.199–205, and cf. Varro (cited by Servius, *ad A.* 5.295), who gives both four and five; Néraudau (1984, 21–38) gives further sources.

5. Jachmann 1952, 56: "der Einschub der sechs verse wirkt wie der Sturz eines mächtigen Felsblocks in einem stillen Dorfweiher er sprengt alles auseinander."

led some critics to conclude that the boy must be metaphoric, a symbol for Rome, perhaps, and that his "life" must represent centuries of progress, decline, and final recovery.[6] If that is the case, the poem's conclusion takes us completely away from the point:

> incipe, parve puer, risu cognoscere matrem
> (matri longa decem tulerunt fastidia menses).

[Begin, small boy, to acknowledge your mother with a smile (ten months brought her long discomfort).]

(Ecl. 4.60–61)

Why recall the particulars of the mother's pregnancy and confirm the boy's ordinary, physical reality, just when we should be assured that he is an abstraction? Vergil's prayer, furthermore, at the end of the poem makes difficult sense if the poet is asking to witness centuries of world ages:

> o mihi tum longae maneat pars ultima vitae,
> spiritus et quantum sat erit tua dicere facta.

[If only then the last part of a long life remain to me, and strength enough to sing your deeds.]

(Ecl. 4.53–54)

We do better to understand the boy as real and the ages as metaphoric; we can now ask what this "epic age" might mean.

Vergil's epic age is not quite an iron age, though it shares some details with those of Hesiod and Aratus,[7] nor does it fit any of the other conventional ages of man. The *Argo*, Troy, and Achilles are too particular and too cataclysmic to be simple shorthand for "the world will briefly decline"; they suggest apocalyptic events and point, moreover, to a version of apocalypse that Vergil alludes to throughout the *Eclogue*: Catullus 64.[8]

---

6. See Norden 1924, especially 44–46, for the Greek and Egyptian versions of this metaphor. A human lifetime is a common symbol for cultural evolution. Seneca (quoted by Lactantius, at *Div. Inst.* 7.15) uses it of Roman history: Rome had her infancy at the time of Romulus, her adolescence under Tarquin, and adulthood during the Punic wars; after the fall of Carthage came Rome's old age, called by Seneca a second childhood. Cf. Ammianus Marcellinus, *Res Gestae* 14.6.4–5, who compares Roman history to the ages of man, and Fulgentius (*Vergiliana Continentia*), who interprets the *Aeneid* as an allegory of a human lifetime. For further bibliography see Coleiro 1979, 220–23.

7. Conington (1963, *ad Ecl.* 4.34) lists the discrepancies.

8. The most obvious allusion is to Catullus' refrain: *currite ducentes subtegmina, currite, fusi;* cf. *Ecl.* 4.46. Herrmann (1930, 62–66) collects other verbal echoes.

The metonymy *Thetis* for *mare* (first here in Latin and perhaps Vergil's invention),[9] the "delectos heroas" of the Argo, and the deeds of Achilles, as the start of a new and corrupt age, comprise a summary of Catullus' epyllion, and Vergil invokes Catullus' idiosyncratic link between heroic characters and deeds and the "iron age" necessities of fortifications, commerce, and agriculture. For Catullus, the first ship, the birth of Achilles, and Troy do not simply characterize an "age" or belong to mythical antiquity; they mark the beginning of the fallen world that Catullus himself inhabits, and they represent the everyday realities (as Catullus describes them) of Lesbia, betrayal, and loss, in heroic dress. Vergil appropriates Catullus' view of life in the modern world and likewise Catullus' assimilation of the "heroic" past to his own time: Vergil makes Tiphys and the Argo emblems for seafaring and commerce, inevitable features of civilization (his own and the boy's), like walls and agriculture; he makes Achilles and Troy metonymic, epic synonyms for the treachery and suffering of the (Catullan) world, the recurring symptoms of *prisca fraus*.[10]

Vergil's epic age, therefore, denotes adult reality, the adversities that the boy (like every boy) will face when he becomes a man. This section of the poem is unintelligible if it describes the appearance (for a decade or so) of a mythical iron age or an age of heroes; it is simple and clear if it is about the growing perception of the real world (in Catullan terms) that accompanies maturation. The boy of the *Eclogue* faces the realities that all children—Ariadne in Catullus 64, the *virgo* in Catullus 65, the *pueri* in the *Aeneid*—confront when they move beyond the illusions of childhood. *Prisca fraus*, the motive force behind legendary Troy and the contemporary civil wars, continues to afflict successive generations;[11] *fraus* does not erupt suddenly in paradise but has been there all along, unperceived in the golden age of childhood, and known only secondhand to the growing boy (lines 26–27, quotation follows).

If this is correct, the golden age (lines 18–25) is childhood itself or, more precisely, the world perceived through the child's eyes: he sees, appropriately, only milk, flowers, and fragrant plants about his *cunabula*:

---

9. Swanson 1967, 324–55, and Coleman 1977, *ad loc.*

10. Cf. especially Catullus 64.347–55, 68.89–104, and chapter 2.

11. A constant refrain in Catullus; compare elsewhere in Vergil, e.g., *G.* 1.501–2: *satis iam pridem sanguine nostro / Laomedonteae luimus periuria Troiae* [Surely by now we have paid enough in blood for the lies of Laomedon's Troy].

> ipsae lacte domum referent distenta capellae
> ubera, nec magnos metuent armenta leones;
> ipsa tibi blandos fundent cunabula flores.
> occidet et serpens, et fallax herba veneni
> occidet; Assyrium vulgo nascetur amomum.

[The goats of their own accord will bring home udders full of milk, and the herds will no longer fear lions; your cradle will bloom with pleasing flowers. The snake will die, and the plant, full of hidden poison, will die; Assyrian cardamon will flourish everywhere.]

(*Ecl.* 4.21–25)

Again, Vergil describes not a world literally transformed but the child's vision, an illusion of security and plenty in a landscape whose dangers (for the present) go unrecognized.

This interpretation depends on the intervening passage (lines 26–30): the five lines are a single sentence, separated from what precedes by *at* and from what follows by *tamen* (line 31), and they are a distinct unit according to the numerical divisions of the poem.[12] Vergil blends elements of the golden age and the epic age in order to mark the boy's progress from child to man:

> at simul heroum laudes et facta parentis
> iam legere et quae sit poteris cognoscere virtus,
> molli paulatim flavescet campus arista
> incultisque rubens pendebit sentibus uva
> et durae quercus sudabunt roscida mella.

[But as soon as you can read the praises of heroes and the deeds of your father and learn what manhood is, then little by little the field will grow golden with ripe wheat, and grapes will redden as they hang among unchecked brambles, and the hard oaks will drip honey like dew.]

(*Ecl.* 4.26–30)

In the first two lines the transition is clearly depicted: *heroum laudes* and *virtus* have no place in the golden age, and the boy only begins to perceive them as he approaches adulthood. He is between "ages," reading about his father's deeds and learning the conventions of heroic manhood (*quae sit . . . virtus*), but still too young to act. For the boy, as for Iulus in his "training" period (*A.* 5–8), and for Pallas asking Aeneas about his *facta* as they sail down the Tiber, the heroic world still appears real (cf. the *lusus*

---

12. Skutsch (1969) divides the middle twenty-eight lines of the poem into eight plus eleven plus nine; the middle eleven fall into five plus six.

Troiae), and *virtus* is a glorious thing; like the details of the *lusus* that reveal heroism to be an illusion, here *virtus* will mean the struggles amid *scelera* and *fraus* of a world in decline.[13]

Vergil subordinates the first two lines to the next three; their simultaneity, *simul [ac]*, is odd and irrelevant unless we understand their thematic connection. As the boy becomes aware of *virtus* and the larger world, his perception of nature also changes. Though the landscape contains typical golden age details (grapes and wheat seem to grow *sua sponte*, and honey drips from trees), there are differences from the golden age of childhood, and these differences parallel the transition of the two previous lines. The infant perceives only a fragrant world of milk and exotic plants, unaware of any danger. The maturing boy still perceives his world as a golden age but in an increasingly real landscape that suggests future *labor*. The milk, honey, and flowers of infancy give way gradually (*paulatim*) to agriculture: wheat may grow spontaneously but presumably cannot be eaten without work; grapes grow among brambles that do not need to be cut back (*incultis*)—but why are there brambles at all, and why grapes instead of wine in the rivers? In the *Georgics* Jupiter's iron age begins with the need for viticulture (and for all other kinds of agriculture): *[Iupiter] passim rivis currentia vina repressit* [(Jupiter) stopped the wine flowing freely in the streams] (G. 1.132); he adds poison to serpents (G. 1.129), and causes *improbus labor* to afflict the world (G. 1.145–46). With these intimations of future *labor* the boy moves away from childhood's paradise and toward an adulthood in which these early intimations will be realized: *pauca tamen suberunt priscae vestigia fraudis / . . . quae iubeant telluri infindere sulcos* [traces of ancestral treachery will nevertheless remain . . . which bid us cut furrows in the earth] (lines 31–33).

I have defined these three sections in the center of the poem as evolving perceptions of reality, childhood illusions that dissolve as the boy grows up to confront civilization and struggle. In the *Aeneid* Vergil returns, though less schematically, to these stages of life. Euryalus leaves his mother and the security of childhood for adult warfare and a heroism debased by darkness and deception (a second *Doloneia*). Pallas leaves his father and the cultural innocence of Pallanteum to enter the war in Latium, a war associated with Troy, Laomedon, and the rest, all the liabilities and constraints of civilization. Iulus' growth repeats the *Eclogue*'s pattern more fully: he develops from an "infant" in Venus' bucolic sanctuary and in Dido's lap, to a *puer* hunting and imitating heroic deeds,

---

13. See "The *lusus Troiae*" in chapter 5, and Ross 1975, 13–14, for *virtus* in Catullus.

until finally he appears as a youth besieged in a new Troy and caught in the labyrinth of the past—a past demythologized and recast by Vergil, as by Catullus, to define contemporary Rome and all ages, the reality of life.

Aeneas' final words to Iulus paraphrase this transitional section of the *Eclogue*: Iulus, like the boy of the *Eclogue*, is enjoined to learn *virtus* and *labor* from his father's deeds. The passage concludes, as I have previously discussed, with a fantasy of deliverance, a father's illusion that he has not endured the "iron age" or "heroic" struggles of adulthood for nothing: he has relived *Odyssey* and *Iliad* (like the *Eclogue* child's adult experience), and despite his own suffering and loss, promises Iulus a better legacy: *mea dextera . . . magna inter praemia ducet.*[14]

The final age in the fourth *Eclogue* (lines 37–45) is a comparable illusion, and the golden age returns, a composite of traditional details, *omnis feret omnia tellus* [the earth will produce all things everywhere] (line 39), and less conventional miracles:

> nec varios discet mentiri lana colores,
> ipse sed in pratis aries iam suave rubenti
> murice, iam croceo mutabit vellera luto;
> sponte sua sandyx pascentis vestiet agnos

[Nor will wool learn to feign different colors, but the ram himself in the meadow will change his coat, now with purple reddening wondrously, now with saffron; with no bidding, scarlet will cloak the grazing lambs.]
(*Ecl.* 4.42–45)

Dyeing and murex traditionally belong to the *luxuria* of the iron age (or some other degenerate state).[15] Here they emerge spontaneously in nature, a peculiarly adult fantasy of paradise, as we might expect if ages are views of reality that evolve in the course of a human lifetime. Multicolored sheep are an arguably frivolous climax to a list that begins with the cessation of seafaring, agriculture, and warfare,[16] and here fantasy is the point, as the traditional features of paradise fade into insubstantial delusion.

---

14. See "*Facta Heroum*" in chapter 5.

15. Coleman (1977, *ad Ecl.* 4.42), compares Lucretius *R.N.* 5.1423, Tibullus 2.4.28, and Vergil *G.* 2.465; for discussion compare Putnam 1970b, 153–55, and B. Thornton 1988.

16. Servius (*ad loc.*) notes a similar Etruscan prophecy, cited more fully by Macrobius (*Sat.* 3.7.2); whether this is in Vergil's mind or not, the view of T. E. Page (1974, *ad loc.*) is hard to resist: "There is only a step from the sublime to the ridiculous and Vergil has here decidedly taken it."

The return of the golden age further mirrors a similar prophetic assertion to Pollio at the beginning of the poem:

> te duce, si qua manent sceleris vestigia nostri
> inrita perpetua solvent formidine terras.
> ille deum vitam accipiet divisque videbit
> permixtos heroas et ipse videbitur illis,
> pacatumque reget patriis virtutibus orbem.

[Pollio, with you as consul, if any traces of our crime remain, they, rendered powerless, will free the earth from fear. That boy will inherit the
life of the gods and will look on heroes mingling with the gods, and he
himself will be seen by them, and he will rule a world pacified by his
ancestors' struggles.]

(Ecl. 4.15–17)

The praises of heroes and the father's deeds that the boy learned by
watching and reading (*laudes heroum, facta parentis,* lines 26–27) are in fact
the struggles to pacify the world, *pacatumque reget patriis virtutibus orbem*
(line 17); the golden age of later life is the illusion that one has succeeded.
The emergence of treachery in the boy's life (*vestigia fraudis*) recapitulates
the persistence of crime in Pollio's consulship (*sceleris vestigia*) and implies a pattern: the consul's success and the ensuing golden age of lines
18–25 were illusions (for both him and the *puer*), and the miseries and
necessities of real life, unchanged, will continue to afflict the boy's generation; so the boy will grow up to share the same belief in the end of
labor and in *luxuria* with impunity in a pacified world.

Saeculum venturum

The preceding reading accounts only for the ages in the middle of the
poem, and we are still a step away from an interpretation of the whole.
The *Eclogue* begins and ends (lines 4–17 and 48–59) with credible expressions of hope, with none of the ambiguities that the progression of ages
contains, and it is surely wrong to dismiss these sections as a false "surface" through which we see Vergil's "real" meaning.

The poem opens with a catalog of prophetic and literary traditions of
paradise:

> Ultima Cumaei venit iam carminis aetas;
> magnus ab integro saeclorum nascitur ordo.
> iam redit et virgo, redeunt Saturnia regna,
> iam nova progenies caelo demittitur alto.

tu modo nascenti puero, quo ferrea primum
desinet ac toto surget gens aurea mundo,
casta fave Lucina: tuus iam regnat Apollo.

[Now the final age of the Sibylline prophecy has come; the great succession of centuries begins anew. Now Virgo returns to earth, now the Saturnian age returns, now a new offspring descends from the heavens. Lucina, show favor to the newborn boy, with whom the iron race will straightway end and the golden race will rise up throughout the world: now your brother Apollo rules.]

(*Ecl.* 4.4–10)

Vergil combines Sibylline prophecies in line 4 with suggestions of both the Stoic *periodos* and the Etruscan *saecula* in line 5, with the literary ages of Aratus and Hesiod (line 6), and finally (perhaps) with the Orphic ages in line 10. Bewildering variety is the point of this section; securely identifying all these doctrines, or finding some schema to make them compatible, is neither possible nor necessary. Vergil blends all the formal expressions of hope that poetry and religion provide, the incompatible and contradictory ways in which people dream about recompense and consolation for despair and suffering, even for civil war, and for the iron age of daily life.[17]

Despite their variety none of these traditions includes a miraculous (human) child as an agent of change;[18] Vergil subsumes this composite of

17. Vergil need not have looked far for his models; prophecy was a flourishing trade at the end of the Republic, so much so that Augustus burned two thousand texts at the time he purged the Sibylline books of interpolations (Suetonius *Div. Aug.* 31); for discussion see Du Quesnay 1976, 75–81. For contemporary numismatic iconography (of the coming golden age) see Alfoldi 1930 and, generally, Syme 1939, 217–20.

18. Coleman 1977, *ad Ecl.* 4.7: "Vergil cannot have found the motif in Graeco-Roman literary sources." The search for this motif among still more arcane sources (e.g., Norden 1924) seems to lead to as many problems as it solves; Du Quesnay (1976) concludes a sensible discussion of similarities of the *Eclogue* to the Book of Isaiah: "This can only be speculation and leads nowhere" (77).
This child is surely closer to hand, and it seems perverse to deny that the poem records contemporary responses to a real birth, most likely the anticipated child of Antony and Octavia (Clausen 1982 and n. 3 in this chapter); to record, it should be needless to say, need not mean to endorse or to credit the hopes that must have bloomed (however briefly) at the truce between Rome's two chief rivals. Asinius Gallus, Pollio's son, claimed that he was the child Vergil intended, though he was in fact born too early for his claim to be true (Coleman 1977, 150). To some critics his assertion suggests that Romans had forgotten, within one generation of the poem's publication, what child Vergil meant—a suggestion that I, with others, find incredible. The addressee of such a *genathlicon*, especially if written for Octavian's "nephew," could scarcely have been forgotten so thoroughly as to produce the bewilderment we find already in Servius, who, by line 13, *te*

traditions under a single theme: childhood and posterity are a perpetual source of hope, more credible and more immediate than cyclical ages or oracular fantasies of deliverance. What has childhood meant elsewhere in Vergil's work and what does it mean to his contemporaries, or to any age, perhaps, that survives decades like those of Rome's civil wars? It was a recurring dream among Romans that their past could be nullified (*in-rita*), and that their endemic *scelera* would at last be paid for (see again Vergil's prayer at the end of the first *Georgic*, lines 491–502):[19] their off-spring would then inherit a world perfected by their wars and sacrifices. Vergil borrows the conventions of the iron age, of the golden age, and of prophecies of redemption to describe his contemporaries' hopes (which persist), and their struggles and failures (which also persist); the theme of the poem is hope itself, defined as an illusion. This is the song of the Parcae, *talia saecla suis dixerunt currite fusis* (46): the cycle of illusion, disillusionment, and the return to illusion again, in every lifetime. The child is not miraculous and he will not change the world, and the riddle of the poem is not his identity but his universality: he is every *puer*, every *iuvenis*, and every *vir*, in a world without change.

---

duce, has abandoned all hope of sorting out Vergil's players: *vel Auguste, vel Pollio, vel Salonine*. Those who understood the poem knew that *no* particular child was addressed: that was the key to its riddle and the reason behind the complete absence of any prevailing contemporary identification.

19. See chapter 5 n. 32.

BIBLIOGRAPHY

Alföldi, A. 1930. Die neue Weltherrscher der vierten Ekloge Vergils. *Hermes* 65:1–30.

Alper, P. 1979. *The Singer of the Eclogues.* Berkeley.

Anderson, W. S. 1969. *The Art of the Aeneid.* New Jersey: Prentice Hall.

Ariès, P. 1962. *Centuries of Childhood: A Social History of Family Life.* Translated from French by R. Baldick. Harmondsworth.

Austin, R. G. 1955. *P. Vergili Maronis Aeneidos Liber Quartus.* Oxford.

———. 1964. *P. Vergili Maronis Aeneidos Liber Secundus.* Oxford.

———. 1971. *P. Vergili Maronis Aeneidos Liber Primus.* Oxford.

Baker, R. 1985. *Regius Puer:* Ascanius in the *Aeneid.* In *Essays in Honor of J. H. Bishop,* 129–45.

Beckett, S. 1978. *Poèmes.* Paris.

Bellen, H. 1963. Adventus Dei. *RhM,* n.s., 106:23–30.

Bettini, M. 1991. *Anthropology and Roman Culture: Kinship, Time, Images of the Soul.* Translated from Italian by John Van Sickle. Baltimore and London.

Binder, G. 1971. *Aeneas und Augustus: Interpretationen zum 8. Buch der Aeneis.* Beitr. zur klass. Phil. 38. Meisenheim.

Bloch, A. 1970. Arma virumque als heroische Leitmotiv. *MH* 27:206–11.

Block, E. 1980. The Failure to Thrive. *Ramus* 9:128–49.

Bömer, F. 1969–83. *P. Ovidius Naso, Metamorphosen,* Wissenschaftliche Kommentare zu lateinischen und griechischen Schriftstellern, vols. 1–4.

Boyd, B. W. 1983. Cydonea mala: Virgilian word-play and allusion. *HSCP* 87:169–74.

Bradley, K. R. 1987. Dislocation in the Roman Family. *Historical Reflections/Réflexions historiques* 14:33–62.

Bremmer, J. 1978. Heroes, Rituals, and the Trojan War. *Studi Storico-Religiosi* 2:5–38.

———. 1983. The Importance of Maternal Uncle and Grandfather in Archaic and Classical Greece and Early Byzantium. *ZPE* 50:173–86.

Briggs, W. W. 1980. *Narrative and Simile from the Georgics in the Aeneid.* Mnem. Suppl. 58. Leiden.

Brunt, P. A. 1987. *Italian Manpower.* Oxford.

———. 1988. *The Fall of the Roman Republic and Related Essays.* Oxford.

Buchheit, V. 1963. *Vergil über die Sendung Roms: Untersuchungen zum Bellum Poenicum und zur Aeneis.* Gymn. Beiheft 3. Heidelberg.

Bühler, W. 1960. *Die Europa des Moschos. Hermes* Einzelschr. 13. Wiesbaden.

Camps, W. A. 1966. *Propertius Elegies Book III.* Cambridge.

Clausen, W. 1970. Catullus and Callimachus. *HSCP* 75:85-94.

———. 1977. Ariadne's Leave-taking. *ICS* II:219-23.

———. 1982. Theocritus and Virgil. In *The Age of Augustus,* ed. E. J. Kenney and W. V. Clausen. *The Cambridge History of Classical Literature* II. 3. Cambridge.

———. 1987. *Virgil's Aeneid and the Tradition of Hellenistic Poetry.* Berkeley, Los Angeles, and London.

Coleiro, E. 1979. *An Introduction to Vergil's Bucolics.* Amsterdam.

Coleman, R. 1977. *Vergil: Eclogues.* Cambridge.

Commager, S. 1983. The Structure of Catullus 62. *Eranos* 81:21-33.

Conington, J. 1963. *The Works of Vergil* with a commentary by J. Conington and H. Nettleship. Hildesheim. Reprint of 1883-84 London edition.

Conte, G. B. 1986. *The Rhetoric of Imitation: Genre and Poetic Memory in Virgil and Other Latin Poets.* Ithaca and London.

Corbier, M. 1991. Divorce and Adoption as Roman Familial Strategies (Le divorce et l'adoption "en plus"). In *Marriage, Divorce, and Children in Ancient Rome,* edited by E. Rawson, 47-78. Oxford.

Dixon, S. 1985. *The Roman Mother.* London and Sydney.

———. 1991. The Sentimental Ideal of the Roman Family. In *Marriage, Divorce, and Children in Ancient Rome,* edited by E. Rawson, 99-113. Oxford.

Dodds, E. R. 1973. *The Ancient Concept of Progress.* Oxford.

Duckworth, G. 1967. The Significance of Nisus and Euryalus for *Aeneid* IX-XII. *AJP* 88:129-50.

Du Quesnay, I. M. LeM. 1976. Vergil's Fourth *Eclogue. Papers of the Liverpool Latin Seminar. ARCA* 2: 25-99.

Eckert, C. W. 1963. Initiation Motifs in the Telemachus Episode. *CJ* 59:49-57.

Edwards, M. 1960. The Expression of Stoic Ideas in the *Aeneid. Phoenix* 14:151-65.

Elder, J. P. 1951. Notes on Some Conscious and Subconscious Elements in Catullus' Poetry. *HSCP* 60:101-36.

Eyben, E. 1993. *Restless Youth in Ancient Rome.* London and New York.

Fedeli, P. 1981. *Catullus Carmen 61.* Amsterdam.

Feeney, D. 1986. History and Revelation in Vergil's Underworld. *PCPS* 32:1-24.

———. 1991. *The Gods in Epic: Poets and Critics of the Classical Tradition.* Oxford.

Feldman, L. H. 1953. The Character of Ascanius in Vergil's *Aeneid. CJ* 48:303-13.

Fitzgerald, G. J. 1972. Nisus and Euryalus: A Paradigm of Futile Behaviour and the Tragedy of Youth. In *Cicero and Virgil: Studies in Honor of Harold Hunt,* edited by J. R. C. Martyn, 114-37. Amsterdam.

Forbiger, A. 1872-75. *Virgili Maronis Opera.* 4th ed. 3 vols. Leipzig.

Fordyce, C. J. 1961. *Catullus.* Oxford.

———. 1977. *P. Vergili Maronis Aeneidos Libri VII-VIII with a Commentary.* Edited by John D. Christie. Oxford.

Fowler, W. W. 1919. *The Death of Turnus.* Oxford.

Fraenkel, E. 1926. *Die Stellung des Römertums in der Humanistischen Bildung.* Berlin.

————. 1945. Some Aspects of the Structure of *Aeneid* VII. *JRS* 35:1–14. Reprinted in *Kleine Beiträge zur klassischen Philologie*, 145–71. Rome, 1964.

————. 1955. *Vesper Adest* (Catullus LXII). *JRS* 45:1–8. Reprinted in *Kleine Beiträge zur klassischen Philologie*, 87–101. Rome, 1964.

————. 1961. Two Poems of Catullus. *JRS* 51:46–53. Reprinted *Kleine Beiträge zur klassischen Philologie*, 115–29. Rome, 1964.

Fränkel, H. 1951. Key-Lines (A.VIII, 185–89) for the Cacus Episode in the *Aeneid*. *Miscellania G. Galbiati* 25:127–28.

Galinsky, K. 1972. *The Herakles Theme*. Oxford.

————. 1988. The Anger of Aeneas. *AJP* 109:321–48.

Gransden, K. W. 1976. *Virgil: Aeneid Book VIII*. Cambridge.

Griffin, J. 1977. The Epic Cycle and the Uniqueness of Homer. *JHS* 97:39–53.

————. 1979. The Fourth *Georgic*, Virgil, and Rome. *GR* 26:61–80.

————. 1986. *Homer on Life and Death*. Oxford.

Hallet, J. 1984. *Fathers and Daughters in Roman Society*. Princeton.

Hardie, P. R. 1986. *Virgil's Aeneid: Cosmos and Imperium*. Oxford.

————. 1994. *Virgil Aeneid Book IX*. Cambridge.

Heinze, R. 1915. *Virgils epische Technik*. 3rd ed. Leipzig-Berlin.

————. 1993. *Virgil's Epic Technique*. Translated from German by H. Harvey and D. Harvey.

Henry, J. 1873–92. *Aeneidea, or Critical, Exegetical, and Aesthetical Remarks on the Aeneid*. 5 vols. Dublin and London.

Herrmann, L. 1930. Le poème 64 de Catulle et Virgile. *REL* 8:211–21.

Herter, H. 1961. Das Leben ein Kinderspiel. *Bonner Jahrbucher* 161:73–84. Reprinted in *Kleine Schriften*, 584–97. Munich, 1975.

————. 1975. Das unschuldige Kind. In *Kleine Schriften*, 598–619. Munich. Originally published in *Jahrbuch für Antike und Christentum* 4:146–62.

Heubeck, A. 1974. *Die Homerische Frage*. Darmstadt.

Heurgon, J. 1931. Un exemple peu connu de la retractatio Vergilienne. *REL* 9:250–68.

Heyne, C. G. 1830–42. *P. Virgili Maronis Opera*. 4th ed., revised by G. P. E. Wagner. 5 vols. Leipzig.

Holt, P. 1980. *Aeneid* V: Past and Future. *CJ* 75:110–21.

Hopkins, K. 1983. *Death and Renewal*. Cambridge.

Hornsby, R. 1970. *Patterns of Action in the Aeneid*. Iowa City.

Hunt, J. W. 1973. *Forms of Glory*. Carbondale, Ill.

Jachmann, G. 1952. Die vierte Ekloge Virgils. *Annali della Scuola Normale Superiore di Pisa* 21:40–62.

Johnson, W. R. 1976. *Darkness Visible: A Study of Vergil's Aeneid*. Berkeley and Los Angeles.

Kassel, R. 1951. *Quo modo quibus locis apud veteres scriptores Graecos infantes atque parvuli pueri inducantur describantur commemorentur*. Ph.D. diss., Mainz.

Kellum, B. 1981. *Sculptural Programs and Propaganda in Augustan Rome: the Temple of Apollo on the Palatine and the Forum of Augustus.* Ph.D. diss., Harvard University.

Kenney, E. J. 1982. Vergil and the Elegiac Sensibility. *ICS* VIII.1 44–52.

Klingner, F. 1940. Über die Dolonie. *Hermes* 75:337–68. Reprinted in *Studien zur griechischen und römischen Literatur,* 7–39. Zurich, 1964.

———. 1956. Catulls Peleus-Epos. *SBAW* 6:1–92. Reprinted in *Studien zur griechischen und römischen Literatur,* 156–224. Zurich, 1964.

———. 1967. *Virgil: Bucolica, Georgica, Aeneis.* Zurich and Stuttgart.

Knauer, G. N. 1964. *Die Aeneis und Homer: Studien zur poetischen Technik mit Listen der Homerzitate in der Aeneis.* Hypomnemata 7. Göttingen.

Knight, W. F. J. 1967. *Vergil: Epic and Anthropology.* London.

Knox, B. M. W. 1950. The Serpent and the Flame. *AJP* 71:379–400.

Kosthorst, A. 1934. *Die Frauen- und Junglingsgestalten in Virgils Aeneas.* Munich.

Kroll, W. 1968. *Catull.* 5th ed. Leipzig.

Last, H. 1934. The Social Policy of Augustus. *Cambridge Ancient History* 10:461–64.

Lee, M. O. 1980. *Fathers and Sons in Vergil's Aeneid.* Albany, N.Y.

Lennox, P. F. 1977. Vergil's Night-Episode Re-examined (*Aeneid* IX, 176–449). *Hermes* 105:331–42.

Lonis, R. 1979. *Guerre et religion en Grèce à l'époque classique.* Paris.

Lyne, R. O. A. M. 1970. *Ciris: A Poem Attributed to Vergil.* Cambridge.

———. 1983. Vergil and the Politics of War. *CQ* 33:188–203.

———. 1987. *Further Voices in Vergil's Aeneid.* Oxford.

———. 1989. *Word and the Poet.* Oxford.

Manson, M. 1978. *Puer Bimulus* (Catulle, 17, 12–13) et l'image du petit enfant chez Catulle et ses prédécesseurs. *Mélanges de l'École Française de Rome: Antiquité* 90:247–91.

———. 1983. The Emergence of the Small Child in Rome (Third Century B.C.– First Century A.D.). *History of Education* 12:149–59.

McLoughlin, T. 1968. An Unusual Offer to Nisus. *PACA* 11:55–58.

Mendell, C. W. 1951. The Influence of the Epyllion on the *Aeneid. YCS* 12:205–26.

Moskalew, W. 1982. *Formular Language and Poetic Design in the Aeneid.* Mnem. Suppl. 73. Leiden.

Mynors, R. A. B. 1972. *P. Vergili Maronis Opera.* 2nd ed. Oxford.

———. 1990. *Virgil: Georgics.* Oxford.

Néraudau. J. 1984. *Être Enfant à Rome.* Paris.

Nicolet, C. 1988. *The World of the Citizen in Republican Rome.* Berkeley and Los Angeles.

Nisbet, R. G. M., and M. Hubbard. 1970. *A Commentary on Horace: Odes Book I.* Oxford.

Norden, E. 1924. *Die Geburt des Kindes: Geschichte einer religiösen Idee.* Leipzig.

———. 1957. *P. Vergilius Maro Aeneis Buch VI,* 4th ed. Stuttgart.

———. 1966. Vergils Aeneis im Lichte ihrer Zeit. In *Kleine Schriften,* 358–421. Berlin. Reprinted from *Njb* 7 (1901): 249–82, 313–34.

O'Hara, J. J. 1990. *Death and the Optimistic Prophecy in Vergil's Aeneid*. Princeton.

Otis, B. 1963. *Virgil: A Study in Civilized Poetry*. Oxford.

Page, T. E. 1974. *P. Vergili Maronis: Bucolica et Georgica*. London.

Pease, A. S. 1935. *P. Vergili Maronis Aeneidos Liber Quartus*. Cambridge, Mass.

Philips, J. 1978. Roman Mothers and the Lives of their Adult Daughters. *Helios* 6:69–80.

Putnam, M. 1962. Unity and Design in *Aeneid* V. *HSCP* 66:205–39.

———. 1965. *The Poetry of the Aeneid: Four Studies in Imaginative Unity and Design*. Cambridge, Mass.

———. 1970a. Catullus 66.75–88. *CP* 65:223–27.

———. 1970b. *Vergil's Pastoral Art*. Princeton.

———. 1987. Daedalus, Virgil, and the End of Art. *AJP* 108:173–98.

Quinn, K. 1968. *Vergil's Aeneid: A Critical Description*. Ann Arbor.

———. 1970. *Catullus: The Poems*. London.

Raabe, H. 1974. *Plurima Mortis Imago: Vergleichende Interpretationen zur Bildersprache Vergils*. Zetemata 59. Munich.

Renehan, R. 1979. New Evidence for the Variant in *Iliad* 1.5. *AJP* 100:473–74.

Ross, D. O. 1969. *Style and Tradition in Catullus*. Cambridge.

———. 1975. *Backgrounds to Augustan Poetry: Gallus, Elegy, and Rome*. Cambridge.

———. 1987. *Virgil's Elements: Physics and Poetry in the Georgics*. Princeton.

Schadewaldt, W. 1965. *Von Homers Welt und Werk*. Stuttgart.

Scheinberg, S. 1982. *Labor and Fortuna in the Aeneid*. Ph.D. diss., Harvard University.

Schlunk, R. 1974. *Homeric Scholia and the Aeneid: A Study of the Influence of Ancient Homeric Literary Criticism*. Ann Arbor.

Schneff, H. 1959. Das Hercule-abenteur in Virgils Aeneis. *Gymnasium* 66:250–68.

Segal, C. P. 1966. *Aeternum per saecula nomen*, the golden bough and the tragedy of history: Part II. *Arion* 5:34–72.

Servius. 1881–84. *Commentarii in Vergilii Carmina*. Edited by G. Thilo and H. Hagen. Vols. 1 and 2. Leipzig.

Shackelton Bailey, D. R. 1956. *Propertiana*. Cambridge.

———. 1986. *Tu Marcellus Eris*. *HSCP* 90:199–205.

Skutsch, O. 1969. Symmetry and Sense in the *Eclogues*. *HSCP* 73:153–69.

Smith, P. W. 1980. History and the Individual in Hesiod's Myth of the Races. *CW* 74:145–63.

Smyth, W. R. 1951. *Interpretationes Propertianae* II. *CQ* 45:74–79.

Sowa, C. A. 1984. *Traditional Themes and the Homeric Hymns*. Chicago.

Stahl, H.-P. 1981. Aeneas—An "Unheroic" Hero? *Arethusa* 14:157–77.

Swanson, D. C. 1967. *The Names in Roman Verse*. Madison, Milwaukee, and London.

Syme, Ronald. 1939. *The Roman Revolution*. Oxford.

———. 1979. Pollio, Saloninus, and Salonae. In *Roman Papers*, edited by E. Badian, 1:18–30. Oxford. Reprinted from *CQ* 31 (1937): 39–48.

Taylor, L. R. 1924. *Severi Equitum Romanorum* and Municipal *Severi:* A Study in Pre-Military Training Among the Romans. *JRS* 14:158–71.

———. 1949. *Party Politics in the Age of Caesar.* Berkeley, Los Angeles, and London.

Thomas, R. F. 1979. On a Homeric Reference in Catullus. *AJP* 100:475–76.

———. 1982a. Catullus and the Polemics of Poetic Reference. *AJP* 103:114–64.

———. 1982b. *Lands and Peoples in Roman Poetry: The Ethnographical Tradition.* Cambridge Phil. Soc. Suppl. Vol. 7. Cambridge.

———. 1987. Virgil's Ecphrastic Centerpieces. *HSCP* 87:175–84.

———. 1988a. Tree Violations and Ambivalence in Vergil. *TAPA* 118:261–75.

———. 1988b. *Virgil: Georgics.* Cambridge.

Thornton, A. 1976. *The Living Universe: Gods and Men in Vergil's Aeneid.* Leiden.

Thornton, B. 1988. A Note on Vergil *Eclogue* 4.42–45. *AJP* CIX:226–28.

Treggiari, S. 1991. *Roman Marriage: Iusti Coniuges from the Time of Cicero to the Time of Ulpian.* Oxford.

Veyne, P. 1978. La famille et l'amour sous le Haut-Empire romain. *Annales Économie, Sociétés, Civilisations* 33:35–63.

———. 1987. *A History of Private Life.* Vol. 1, *From Pagan Rome to Byzantium.* Translated from French by A. Goldhammer. Cambridge, Mass., and London.

Vlachos, G. C. 1974. *Les Sociétés Politiques Homériques.* Paris.

Weber, C. 1978. Gallus' Grynium and Virgil's Cumae. *ARCM* 1:45–76.

———. 1987. Metrical *Imitatio* in the Proem to the *Aeneid. HSCP* 91:261–71.

Weinstock, S. 1971. *Divus Julius.* Oxford.

West, M. 1980. *Hesiod: Works and Days.* Oxford.

Westendorp-Boerma, R. E. H. 1958. Vergil's Debt to Catullus. *A. Class.* 1:51–63.

Wetmore, M. N. 1930. *Index Verborum Vergilianus.* New Haven.

Wiedemann, T. 1989. *Adults and Children in the Roman Empire.* New Haven and London.

Wiesen, D. S. 1973. The Pessimism of the Eighth *Aeneid. Latomus* 32:737–65.

Wigodsky, M. 1965. The Arming of Aeneas. *C. & M.* 26:93–221.

———. 1972. *Vergil and Early Latin Poetry. Hermes* Einzelschr. 24. Weisbaden.

Wilamowitz-Moellendorff, U. von. 1924. *Hellenistische Dichtung in der Zeit des Kallimachos.* 2 vols. Berlin.

Wili, W. 1930. *Virgil.* Munich.

Willcock, M. M. 1989. Battle Scenes in the *Aeneid. PCPS,* n.s., 29:94.

Williams, R. 1960. *P. Vergili Maronis Aeneidos Liber Quintus.* Oxford.

Wlosok, A. 1967. *Die Göttin Venus in Vergils Aeneis.* Heidelberg.

Zanker, P. 1983. Der Apollontempel auf dem Palatin: Ausstatung und politische Sinnbezüge nach der Schlacht von Actium. *ARID.* Suppl. 10:21–40.

———. 1988. *The Power of Images in the Age of Augustus.* Ann Arbor.

Zarker, J. W. 1969. Amata: Vergil's Other Tragic Queen. *Vergilius* 12:2–24.

Zetzel, J. E. G. 1978. A Homeric Reminiscence in Catullus. *AJP* 99:332–33.

———. 1989. *Romane Memento:* Justice and Judgment in *Aeneid* 6. *TAPA* 119:263–84.

INDEX LOCORUM

INDEX NOMINUM ET RERUM